FROM HISTORY TO
GENEALOGY PLUS DNA

FROM HISTORY TO GENEALOGY PLUS DNA

Ralph Champion

iUniverse, Inc.
New York Lincoln Shanghai

From History to Genealogy Plus DNA

iUniverse books may be ordered through booksellers or by contacting:

iUniverse
2021 Pine Lake Road, Suite 100
Lincoln, NE 68512
www.iuniverse.com
1-800-Authors (1-800-288-4677)

ISBN: 978-0-595-48252-8 (pbk)
ISBN: 978-0-595-60339-8 (ebk)

Printed in the United States of America

I dedicate this book to the late **John Schroeder** of DeVry University, Irving, Texas. He was a graduate of the West Point Military Academy, had a military career, and was an open, honest, dedicated and effective University Professor. I think he would have enjoyed the military history!

Acknowledgements

The image on the front cover is "Settlers Landing at Jamestown" (in public domain) by Sidney King from The National Park Service's Colonial National Historical Park. Essentially the history of the future United States starts with the Jamestown settlement in 1607. This town contained within itself the seeds of future strife in the United States through the U.S. Civil War.

I thank my first cousin Elizabeth Crouse from Alabama for all the genealogical help she's given me. She sent me a copy of the Bonner Family Bible and shared her personal knowledge of the Bonner family history with me. She also challenged me to follow the Bonner line in England back to the Norman Invasion of 1066. I got lost in the 1500's in England.

Contents

Introduction

The plan of the book was to first cover the history of the southeastern United States where my ancestors lived, and then to look at their genealogy. What happened in the Americas before the Jamestown Virginia Colony was founded was crucial to later history. The Colony started the conquest by the English of what is now the United States and Canada.

In doing research on my family's (Bonner and Champion) genealogical history, I found more interesting material than I expected! The section on genealogy includes the rise of DNA, a valuable tool for history research. My ancestors migrated from England in the 1600's, and continued migrating in southeasterly direction to Alabama and Mississippi. .

The Indians were the barrier to European colonization in the Americas. After being devastated by European-born diseases, the Indians had the choice of fighting the whites or letting themselves be cheated by them. Both things happened!

The French and Indian War set up tensions between England and the colonials that led to the American War of Independence. With help from the French government the colonialists barely won. I've selected a few colonial (and U.S.) incidents not fully understood by Americans.

The Civil War is examined with the idea that, in many ways, it was a continuation of the War with Mexico. The guerrilla aspects were similar to those in other countries, such as in South Vietnam.

Genealogical research was used to develop my Champion (Father) and Bonner (Mother) family trees. DNA testing gave me information on:

- Migration of my ancestors out of Africa 50,000 years ago on the way to England
- Checking an Internet DNA Y-chromosome database for common ancestors

Other uses for DNA are explored:

- DNA fingerprints and DNA forensics
- Medical treatments based on genetic knowledge of the patient
- Prenatal counseling
- Paternity checks
- DNA testing for information for insurance companies and employers

My intentions were to examine key historical events in the southeastern United States. Everything is not always the same as recorded in my High School history books!

Some stories are in poetic form. I have a saga-like poetic style, and use the outline of the poem to make key points stand out. Send your comments to my web site at: golopez@earthlink.net

I. Early Explorations in the Americas

A. *Human Migration to the Americas*

The standard textbooks say that humans (to be called Indians) crossed the Bering Strait to Alaska from Siberia about 13,000 years ago by a "land bridge". This combination of land bridge had only existed once in the last 20,000 years for a few hundred years. It is 58 miles across the Bering Strait at its shortest distance between North America and Siberia. Its water depth is 100-165 feet. Since the level of the Bering Straits waters could fall as much as 350 feet in a really cold ice age, a dry land "bridge" has periodically happened. Siberia from the Bering Straits to the Cherskiy Range belongs to the North American tectonic plate.

The migrants worked their way south through Canada between two great glacial ice sheets to eventually populate all the Americas. DNA evidence finds that American Indians relate most closely to the native peoples of Siberia, not at all to Europeans.

The Clovis culture in Clovis, New Mexico was recognized as settled by these people. The site (earliest was 11,500 years old) was excavated, having a distinctive set of tools, spear-straighteners, hatchet-like choppers, and crescent-moon-shaped objects with unknown functions.

Sites have been found in southern Chile showing human habitation more than 12,000 years old. Perhaps there could have been more than migration from Asia! And the Indians could have utilized canoes to go down the Pacific Coast from Alaska. When I asked my Indian brother-in-law how the Cherokees got to the east coast of the United States, he said: "They used canoes."

Suggested migrations from Asia are: (1) 35,000 BC
(2) 20,000 BC
(3) 13,000 BC
(4) 8,000 BC

But some of the migrants could have come from elsewhere, such as Ainu from Japan and Hispanic people from Spain!

All this is not as upsetting as evidence that early man was in the Americas earlier: There is evidence that Carlos Ameghino found stone tools at the seashore at Miramar, Argentina, suggesting that humans, capable of manufacturing tools and using fire, lived in Argentina 2-3 million years ago in the Late Phocene. Could these people have been "Homo erectus" instead of "Homo sapiens"?

B. *The Europeans' Secret Weapon: Diseases*

The Spaniards couldn't have prevailed in Mexico and Peru against millions of Indians. The Indians were vulnerable to many European diseases such as smallpox, measles, mumps, typhus, influenza, viral hepatitis:

- Within twenty years of Columbus's arrival smallpox had wiped out at least half the people of the West Indies and had started to spread to the South American mainland
- The Indian population of Hispaniola declined by one-third by 1535
- The resulting epidemics killed nearly half the Aztecs
- Smallpox came to Peru overland, killing in 1524-25 200,000, at least of the Inca population
- Of the estimated twenty million Indians living in North America, within a century as many as 95% had died from disease
- Viral hepatitis from 1616-19 killed as much as 90% of the Indians in Coastal New England

Diseases killed 80-100 million Indians for the first third of the 17th century, about 1 out of 5 of everybody on earth!

The American Indians' closest DNA genetic relation was the indigenous Siberians. The Russians' advancing into Siberia caused similar disease epidemics among the natives.

Why were the American Indians so defenseless against European diseases? The Indians had not domesticated large animals such as pigs and cattle, not being exposed to the diseases these animals can pass to humans.

These diseases could pass out into the mainland before the Europeans actually arrived. Portuguese fishermen fishing off Newfoundland passed on diseases with minimal trading contact with the Indians, killing as many as 90% of the Indians.

Are the Europeans at fault for passing these diseases to the Indians? No, because they didn't understand they were "carriers". They were responsable, of course.

"Homo Sapiens" learns quickly. Once they knew what was going on, they used "bioterrorism". In 1346 Tartar forces attacking the city of Kaffa (Caffa east of the Black Sea) by siege catapulted the plague-infected bodies of their own men over the city's walls. Using dead bodies and excrement as weapons continued in Europe during the Black Plague of the 14th and 15th centuries. As late as the early 18th century, Russian troops fighting Sweden catapulted plagued bodies over the city walls of Revel.

Spanish conquistador Pizarro gave clothing contaminated with the smallpox virus to South American natives. Britain's Lord Jeffrey Amherst continued the practice into the late 18th century by having Captain Simeon Ecuyer, a senior officer and Fort Pitt's senior officer, in 1763 infecting native Americans during the French and Indian War by giving them blankets and handkerchiefs that had previously been used at a hospital treating smallpox victims. This killed half the Indian tribe.

Amherst was furious at Pontiac's attacks on British forts at Detroit and Presqu'Isle. There was a similar case in Brazil, and it is suspected that the U.S. Army did similar tricks in the 19th century against certain Indian tribes, especially Plains groups.

In 1491 there were probably more people living in the Americas than in Europe. Between the 16th and 17th centuries Europeans continually lost when they couldn't take a city's walls.

"Syphilis" seems to have developed in the "New World" to be transmitted in the 1500's to Europe by Columbus's men. It seems to have developed in the "New World" from maws about 1,600 years ago.

C. Another Aztec Disease Killer: Cocolitzli

There is another disease native to South America that may have caused killing epidemics among the Aztecs. In 1545 and 1576 epidemics of a malignant form of a hemorrhagic fever appeared in the highlands of Mexico. It lasted three to four days but didn't much affect the Spaniards. The transmission pattern is similar to "hantavirus" that caused "Four Corners Disease", coming after years of drought, followed by much rain.

The Aztecs called it "cocolitzli".

The disease caused incomparable devastation that passed readily from region to region, killing quickly. The illness was characterized by high fever, headaches, bleeding from the nose and ears, accompanied by jaundice, and abdominal and thoracic acute neurological manifestations.

Hemorrhagic fevers are viral diseases that strike with sudden intensity, rarely respond to treatment, kill at high rates, and vanish as mysteriously as they came. They are called hemorrhagic because the victims bleed, hemorrhaging in their capillaries, beneath the skin, and from their noses and ears. The breakdown of the nervous system kills. The diseases' virus is simple compounds only of DNA enveloped in a thin membrane. They develop in an animal host such as rodents or bats. They are spread by insects (such as ticks and mosquitoes) by bites, or through exposure to rodent's feces or urine. Windblown particles can pass the virus to humans. If cocolitzli was caused by a hemorrhagic virus, the Spanish couldn't have brought it with them.

The times of the greatest Aztec plagues were preceded by years of exceptional drought. Such droughts forces rodents to hole up together wherever water is found. In close quarters the viruses were transmitted during bloody fights. Infected mother rodents passed the viruses to their young during pregnancy. When rain returned, the rodents bred quickly and spread the viruses as they came into contact with humans. Humans transmitted the disease among themselves through contact of blood, feces, and saliva.

In 1545-1546 it killed up to eighty percent of the Indian population in Mexico. The epidemic of 1576 killed 45% of the native population. Why didn't it affect the Spanish much? It affects human populations that are already "stressed", such as widespread poverty, poorly clothed, over-worked, and poor nutrition. Also, the Spanish might not have had as much exposure to rodents as the Indians.

D. If the Indians Had Been Immune to European Diseases

Cook and Borah estimated that, when Columbus landed, the central Mexican plateau had a population of 25 million. Spain and Portugal together had only ten million.

Dolyns argued that the Indian population in 1491 was between 90 and 112 million. The United Nations estimated that earth's population at the beginning of the sixteenth century was about 500 million.

Groups like the Narragansetts were spared by the 1616 smallpox epidemic, but were crushed by a smallpox epidemic in 1633. One-third to half the Indians in New England died.

If these epidemics had not happened, the Europeans would have only been able to take and hold islands with their ships and cannons, perhaps even a port or two on the main lands.

II. The Jamestown Colony of Virginia

A. The Charter of the Virginia Company of London

The second Virginia charter was granted at the request of the company May 23, 1609. It created a corporate trading and colonizing company closely analogous to the East India Company:

(1) The company was chartered under the name "The Treasurer and Company of Adventurers and Planters of the City of London for the First Colony in Virginia". It was fully incorporated, with a seal and all legal corporate powers and liabilities. The grant was made to the company in perpetuity, although some of its special exemptions and privileges were for a shorter time only.

(2) The applicable region was the territory stretching four hundred miles along the coast, north and south from Chesapeake Bay, and "up into the land from sea to sea westward and northward". The possession of the soil was given to the company with the requirement that it be distributed by the company to those who contributed money, services or their presence to the colony.

(3) Its commercial powers extended to the exploitation of all the resources of the country with non-company Englishmen paying a subsidy of five per cent of all exported or imported goods, and all foreigners ten per cent.

(4) The company might make all orders, laws, directions, and other provisions necessary for government of the colony. The governor and other officers shall have full and absolute power and authority to correct, punish, pardon, govern, and rule all inhabitants of

the colony in accordance with its laws already made with the said Virginia provinces and sea transit to and from the colony. The governor had the right to use military force. The governor might exercise martial law in the colony.

(5) For seven years the company takes what is necessary for colony government and support and for trade with the natives free of all tax or duty. For twenty years the company was free of customs on goods imported into Virginia, and forever pays only five per cent import duty on goods brought from England to Virginia. All the king's subjects in the colony should be treated the same as if they had remained or been born in England.

(6) For socage tenure on which the land was held, a payment of one-tenth of all gold and sold was required from the company. The members of the council of the company were required to take an oath of allegiance to the king in the name of the company. It was expected that the company should continuously transport colonists.

(7) The company officials should ensure the Protestantism of the settlers before they sailed from England.

(8) The form of government of the company received much attention in the charter. The membership and quarterly assemblies of the general body of members, more frequent meetings of a governing council and their duties were all minutely formulated.

B. Gosnold the Catalyst

One of the most underestimated
Pioneers of the Jamestown Colony
Was explorer Bartholomew Gosnold.

He read law at Cambridge University
But spent a lot of effort studying navigation
And exploration of the New World.

He conversed at Cambridge with
Hakluyt, Drake, and Raleigh
Who wanted to explore the Americas.

He married into a wealthy, influential family,
Captained his own ship, and did pirating–
Oops! privateering on Spanish ships.

Gosnold was the commander of
The expedition to explore
Norumbaga (Vineland).

In 1602 he sailed directly across the
Atlantic Ocean, discovered and named
Cape Cod and Martha's Vineyard.

He tried to find good
Places for English settlement
And get friendly native contact.

Gosnold wanted to settle a permanent
Colony with twenty men, but his
Resources were too inadequate.

Back home he promoted a
Permanent settlement in the Americas
With wealthy English supporters.

He met and recruited Captain
John Smith for leadership and
A strict disciplinary approach.

After Philip of Spain in 1605
Ratified the English peace treaty,
English settlement was practicable.

He played a pivotal role in organizing
The Jamestown Expedition, and securing
A royal charter from King James I.

Gosnold recruited about 50%
Of the original settlers, including
Smith and Wingfield (a neighbor).

Gosnold was selected by the
London Company of Virginia to
Sail one of three expedition ships.

Gosnold lost the argument with Wingfield
On where to implement the colony site,
Claiming that Jamestown was unhealthy.

In all this he was a mover and power;
He lost his claim for fame by dying
In an epidemic in 1607.

Smith caught it too,
But survived to become
The Jamestown leader.

Gosnold was the only original
Jamestown colonist to be buried
With honors and an Admiral's Staff.

Virginia would probably have become
Spanish if not for Gosnold's efforts
In England and Virginia.

The Association for the Preservation of
Virginia Antiquities called him "The Prime
Mover of the colonization of Virginia"!

C. Gosnold: Catalyst to the Jamestown Virginia Colony

Bartholomew Gosnold, an Englishman, was a lawyer, privateer, sea captain, and explorer. Gosnold was about six feet tall, with black hair (a Norman characteristic).

He inspired such bold and resourceful men as Captain John Smith and the Earl of Southampton to pursue colonization in the New World for England. He was born in 1571 and grew up in the valley of the Finn in Suffolk, England (fifty miles northwest of London) at Otley Hall, his family home. He had valuable contacts politically at court, such as his first cousin John Gosnold being Gentleman Usher in Charge of Protocol, and Gentleman of the Privy Chamber.

He attended Cambridge University to study Law. He attended lectures by John Dee and Richard Hakluyt on cartography and geography. He conversed with such men as Richard Hakluyt, Sir Francis Drake, and Sir Walter Raleigh. His goal was exploration in the New World. Marrying Mary Golding gave him entrance to a circle of powerful and wealthy people with the patriotic interest in developing trade and expanding England's sphere of influence in the New World.

He became a privateer (with a license from Queen Elizabeth) and captained his own ship. The English Court took ten percent of the proceeds of privateering. He sailed with Sir Walter Raleigh on several large raids (on Cadiz and the Spanish

West Indies Treasure Fleet). He gained a reputation for good judgment and seamanship. His tidy shares in at least four privateering expeditions gave him the finances to help organize a voyage to the New World in 1602.

In 1600 Queen Elizabeth granted a patent to discover ways and means to trade in the West Indies. Richard Hayluyt, a friend of Gosnold, was appointed Secretary of the East Indies Company. He recommended building small forts or trading stations near the mouths of navigable rivers, these being the forerunners of settlements. Gosnold was selected as Commander of the expedition to explore Norumbega, which the Vikings called Vineland, in what is now called Massachusetts.

In 1602 he sailed the Concord directly across the Atlantic Ocean from England to shorten the trip, rather than detouring by the West Indies. He discovered and named Cape Cod and Martha's Vinyard (named for his daughter).

His goals were to find suitable places for English settlements, and to establish friendly relations with the natives. The expedition was to do soil surveys with experimental planting of crops, collecting valuable minerals, and the observation and classification of flora and fauna. The drawing of charts and maps was based on soundings and observations of the coast line. The stores of the expedition were supposedly enough food to last at least six months. His ship crew traded with natives who had come from the shore in canoes. All the Indians had copper ornaments. Copper was a treasured metal in England. The tobacco the Indians smoked seemed better than that to which the English were accustomed.

Gosnold had already witnessed the fertility of the soil. As Hakluyt suggested, he treated the Indians with respect. He believed the climate in the

New World to be pleasant enough, the summer being longer than the English summer.

Before the first real Thanksgiving, the fort was beginning to take shape, the first English habitation built on the shores of New England at the site of present day Naushon on Elizabeth's Isle in the Elizabeth Islands. The Indians proved to be the friendliest Indians he had met so far in America. Their gifts included food, hemp, rich animal furs, tobacco, cooked turtles, and colored chains.

Gosnold proposed to stay with twenty men and found a permanent colony. He abandoned this because they didn't have enough food to last six months. The number of colonists would have been too low for survivability in cases of illness, food shortages, and warfare with the Indians.

He returned to England with a company of mostly country gentlemen who didn't suffer any serious illness during the entire expedition. He proved that the New World would be a great asset to England in trade and colonization. Gosnold was the first Englishman to set foot on the New England shores, establishing a settlement there.

The voyage was an illegal one as far as Sir Walter Raleigh (who held the patent to make America an English nation) was concerned. Hakluyt, friend of Gosnold, was the guiding spirit behind the expedition. Captain Gosnold was only carrying out the purpose of the patent given to Sir Humphrey Gilbert by the queen in 1578 by exploring Norumbaga. Raleigh gave his belated permission for the Gosnold voyage in exchange for some free publicity. As part of the agreement, Raleigh gave Hakluyt consent to organize another voyage to America, with the support of the Bristol merchants to find more sassafras. Raleigh's position was weakened because of his failures at Roanoke to plant permanent colonies, losing much money and lives.

The new objective included the organization of a state-backed expedition sanctioned by the monarch. Gosnold's discoveries in America complemented almost exactly both Hayes' and Hakluyt's proposals, such as searching for good fishing grounds, the building of small trading stations near the mouths of a great harbor, the finding of grapes and sassafras, and using a shorter sailing route across the Atlantic Ocean.

Gosnold was the pivotal personality of the project. One of his most significant moves was the recruitment of Captain John Smith (who he met in 1605), who was crucial in the future survival of Jamestown with his leadership and strict approach to discipline.

King James I signed the patent for colonizing Virginia after, on June, 1605, Phillip of Spain ratified the peace treaty with England. Now the Spanish would treat the English colonies as legal ventures. This made Raleigh's previous patent obsolete. This document committed the English to plant permanent colonies overseas.

The first company formed was the Plymouth Company, the second the London Company of Virginia. Sir Thomas Smyth was elected Treasurer to the council which had governing rights over the Virginia Company. In November, 1606, sailing instructions were issued with a locked strong box containing the names of the Governing Council (not to be opened until the ships arrived in America). He was instructed to lead a group of men into the interior of the New World to search for minerals such as gold and copper and to for the Northwest Passage.

On December 20, 1606 three small ships left Blackwall, Middlesex, near London: the Susan Constant, the Godspeed (captained by Gosnold), and the Discovery. Captain Christopher Newport was the Admiral and commanded the flagship, the Susan Constant.

Gosnold was Vice-Admiral. On March 23rd, they reached Martinique in the West Indies. On April 10 the fleet turned northerly towards the southeast coast of North America.

On April 26th they sailed into the Chesapeake Bay. That night the box was opened, with Gosnold first on the list, also Captain John Smith's name.

On the selection of the Jamestown site, Gosnold and Wingfield disagreed. Gosnold said the land, despite its easy access, was unsafe and unhealthy. The instructions required access to a fresh water pond or lake. He pleaded for Archer's Point to be selected.

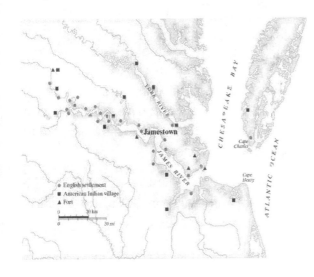

He was overruled with the Council, and Wingfield's decision prevailing. Half the settlers were dead by the end of September, partly due to drinking the contaminated swamp water.

Wingfield was elected the first president of the council, serving for one year.

From the beginning Gosnold had his hands full keeping the peace among the colonists.

President Wingfield decreed there would be no building of fornications or any exercises in the use of arms.

Wowwinchopinck visited Jamestown with 100 armed warriors. Two days later another visit without his presence.

Newport took 23 men, excluding Gosnold but including John Smith's exploring. The day before he returned to Jamestown, hundreds of natives attacked but were fought off. What really rescued the colonists was cannon fire from one of the ships anchored nearby, knocking down a large tree branch, frightening the natives and prompting them to leave. As a result of the hostilities a fort was built.

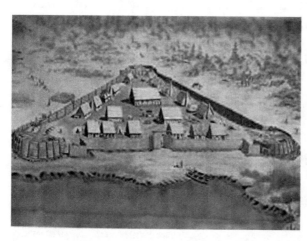

Jamestown Fort

In early August an epidemic of dysentery, caused by drinking the contaminated swamp water started to take its toll. A few days later Gosnold was stricken with fever, dying August 22, 1607 at the age of 36. Captain Smith got sick but recovered, moved into the position of leadership at Jamestown and kept the colony together during trying times.

Gosnold was the only member of the original Jamestown colonists to be buried with full honors. He died too soon to take any bows, but Virginia would probably have become Spanish if not for his efforts!

In an excavation at Jamestown a coffin was found occupied by a skeleton dressed as an Admiral with an Admiral's baton, which Gosnold had in the Jamestown sea journey from England. The rebuilt skull can be seen at

http://www.bbc.co.uk/suffolk/content/articles/2006/03/28/gosnold_feature.shtml

Do you think it's Gosnold after comparing the image to the drawing of Gosnold on page 19? The similarity of the ears convinced me!

D. Captain John Smith's Confinement on the Voyage to Jamestown

A fateful feud began on the Susan Constant while they were waiting for the right winds to get them out of the Channel off England's Kent coast. Edward-Maria Wingfield and some others of high rank were impatient with waiting and were ready to return to their homes. Smith argued against them. The expedition's preacher, the Reverent Robert Hunt, successfully intervened on Smith's side. This kept the fleet from turning around.

By early February the Atlantic journey got under way. Newport sailed south to the Canary Islands off the coast of Africa, then southwest to the Caribbean. Here tempers flared between Smith and Wingfield the day after the three ships left the islands. Smith may have overstepped his social bounds by sharing his opinions with the worthies. In the end he was accused of planning an insurrection. While the charges were trumped up, Wingfield prevailed upon Newport to have Smith placed under arrest on the Susan Constant for the duration of the voyage.

The ships reached the West Indies on March 23 off the island of Martinique. A gallows was built on Nevis for Smith, but he "could not be persuaded to use it". He had "faced down" his adversaries.

On April 16 the ships entered Chesapeake Bay. The sealed orders from the Virginia Company were opened with a list of the seven men who would govern as members of the colony's ruling council. John Smith was one of these! The news of his appointment wasn't enough to set him free yet. Since every hand was needed to prepare the site, the colony's leadership released him from his captivity on the Susan Constant.

Wingfield and unknown others wanted Smith on the ships with Newport when he left for England, but Smith avoided the return trip. Robert Hunt spoke up for Smith, with the respect of both sides. Smith was permitted to take his oath of office and assume his seat on the council.

Wingfield was relieved from his office. Smith brought a suit against him for slander to clear Smith's name of the accusation of mutiny Wingfield had levied against him at the Canary Islands. The twelve jurors awarded Smith 200 pounds. To satisfy the award Wingfield had to give to Smith his private food stocks and other possessions, which Smith donated to the colony's stores for general use.

E The Starving Time at Jamestown

Smith in 1609 was President of the Jamestown colony. He chose to disperse the colonists, putting more food within reach while consolidating the men near (but not in) the Jamestown fort, keeping them safer from attack.

While returning from a trip to quash a mutiny, Smith had his powder bag ignite, giving him a painful injury. It is suspected it wasn't an accident! He returned to England shortly before his term of office as President ended.

After Smith's departure, the colonists told inquiring Indians that Smith was dead. Pocahontas believed this.

Powhatan had his Indians attack the Nansemond settlement. The surviving colonists withdrew to Jamestown for safety. With the collapse of the settlements at the falls and at Nansemond, no one would be foraging there for food that winter of 1609!

All the colony's fishing nets had been allowed to rot. The harvest had been eaten. The storehouse manager told President Percy that there was less than three months of rations left.

The Indians attacked Ratliffe's ship, which had been expected to return to Jamestown loaded with corn. It returned with no food, and with only 16 of the 50 men who had sailed from Jamestown.

West was sent to get grain into his ship from Patawomendas. He got the grain and then sailed for England instead of Jamestown!

Some hungry colonists robbed the storehouse, for which Percy had them executed. As the stores dwindled, the colonists ate the horses, cats, dogs, rats and mice, and the leather of their shoes and boots. A certain amount of cannibalism took place.

By March, 1610, only 60 out of 500 colonists survived, about an 80% mortality rate.

If Percy had adopted an effective defense policy of the outpost settlements at Nansemond and the Falls, things might have been better.

F. Colonial Indentures

The Virginia Company devised the system of indentured servitude in the late 1610's to finance the recruitment and transport of workers from England to the Virginia Colony.

Servitude played a major role in the settlement of the colonies. During the colonial era, some 200,000 to 300,000 servants came to British mainland North America, accounting for ½ to 2/3 of the European immigrants. The doubling of England's population from 2.3 to 4.8 million between 1520 and 1630 was a major force behind immigration, especially among the poorer sections of society who had increased poverty. As much as half the population in towns, cities, and ports lived on or below the poverty line.

Loss of one or both parents was common among poor migrants, and parishes often rid themselves of the expense and trouble of caring for unwanted children by indenturing them for service overseas.

Indenture servitude resembled "service in husbandry", a major source of agricultural labor in early modern England. Servants entered their labor contracts voluntarily, but had little control over the terms or conditions of their labor and living standards. Terms were about four years for skilled adults to ten years or more for unskilled minors. They could be sold without their consent. Their contracts could be extended if they ran away or became pregnant.

The "Master" of the contract transported the servant to the colony, furnished him with adequate food, drink, clothing, and shelter during his service, perhaps even giving the released servant a specified reward when his term was ended. Sometimes a ship captain was the "Master", selling the contracts in the colonies.

The high wages, cheap land, and rapid growth of the colonial economy remained sufficiently enticing to persuade successive generations of immigrants to take the chance and endure the hardships.

There were four forms of immigrant servitude:

(1) servants signed an indenture before departure, which were sold to a master when the servants reached the colonies;

(2) Customary servants were usually younger than those with indentures, and served longer terms;

(3) "Dedemptioners" agreed to pay passage upon arriving in the colonies; if usable to pay, they were sold as servants to satisfy their debt;

(4) Penal servitude became an important source of labor in the 18th century when some 50,000 convicts were shipped to the colonies.

In 1619 the first legislative assembly in America provided for the recording and enforcing of contracts made with servants before their departure from England. To regulate the treatment of indentured servants, each colony evolved a certain standard known as the "Custom of the Country".

Most migrants were male, young, in their late teens and early twenties, traveling alone rather than with family members. In the 17th century they were chiefly English. During the 17th century most of the white laborers in Maryland and Virginia came from England as indentured servants.

Initially servants were concentrated in the staple-producing colonies, such as tobacco in the Chesapeake Bay. Slaves eventually displaced servants. By the early 18th century indentured servants were concentrated in the Mid-Atlantic region in industries requiring particular skills (such as iron-making, shipbuilding, construction, various service trades, and at precision or semiartistic crafts).

Virginia instituted the "Headright System", in which a colonist was granted 50 acres of land for each person's passage to Virginia from England that they paid for.

"Indentured Servitude" resulted in many migrants populating the colonies. Between 1623 and 1637 78% of the immigration to Virginia was indentured. The French in their North American possessions did not have such an influx of settlers. Canada only really got needed migration from the Loyalists during and after the Revolutionary War.

The institution was unimportant in the United States after 1800.

G. John Rolfe: Developed Colony's Cash Crop and Married Pocahontas

John Rolfe sailed to Jamestown from England with his wife and child May, 1609. They had a shipwreck in the Bermudas, and took a year to get new ships to continue north to Jamestown. His daughter died in Bermuda, and his wife died soon after they reached Jamestown.

The colonists had difficulty finding a way to return profits to the Virginia Company in England. The Virginia Indians' tobacco was not as popular in England as that the Spaniards sold in England from the Caribbean. The Spaniards found West Indies natives using the tobacco plant. Rolfe introduced this more fragrant tobacco (Nicotiana tobacco from Trinidad) to Virginia, giving the colonists the "cash crop" they needed. Previously Spain and Portugal monopolized the European tobacco trade, England importing tobacco from Spain. In 1617 Virginia tobacco exports to England were 20,000 pounds, thirteen later it was 1.5 million pounds per year!

Rolfe became enamored of Pocahontas, Chief Powhatan's favorite daughter. She had learned English, and converted to Christianity, being baptized as "Rebecca". He obtained permission to marry her from English officials. Since Chief Powhatan found the match acceptable, they were married 1614 in Virginia. They had a son, Thomas. After the marriage the Chief was friendlier to the colonists than before. The family moved to England in 1616. Due to Rolfe's influence she was introduced to King James I as a princess.

She died that year due to a pulmonary infection, probably caused by the coal-burning in London, which they lived close to. She was buried in Gravesend, England. John returned to Virginia, leaving his ill son (Thomas) in England to be raised by an uncle.

In Virginia he became a councilor and a member of the House of Burgesses. He died March 22, 1622 in the first massacre of the colonists by the Indians. Thomas moved to Virginia in 1640 to be welcomed by his aunt Cleopartre and his great uncle Opekankano, and received an inheritance of thousands of acres of land along the James River from his deceased grandfather Chief Powhatan (Pocahontas' father). Developing this inheritance made him a wealthy plantation owner. He married Jane Polythress in Virginia, having one daughter.

John Rolfe is famous in the history books for marrying Pocahontas, Pocahontas and her son, Thomas Rolfe, giving the colonists peace with the Indians as long as she lived.

As important was then his development of tobacco as Virginia's "cash crop"!

III. Indians

A. The Lost Colony of Virginia

Sir Walter Raleigh wanted to seat the second English colony in the Chesapeake Bay area in order to attain:

(1) a deep-water naval base for attacks on Spanish ships;

(2) many islands for defenses against Indians; and

(3) more arable land than found in the Carolina swamps.

He appointed John White, the artist, as Governor of the incorporated City of Raleigh as a feudal community with an appointed aristocracy and common people to do the heavy work. Unfortunately none of them knew how to fish! They included the Indian chief Mantee, who had become an ally during his stay in England. Unlike the first colony by Ralph Lane (which failed), both sexes and all ages were included.

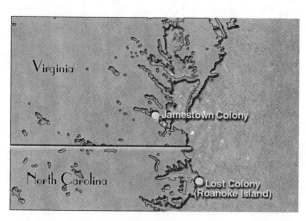

The fleet left Portsmouth on April 26, 1587 with more than 100 colonists on board. The Governor visited the Indians of Croatia and of Cape Hatteras, and the Croaroans. When they arrived at the Roanoke Island (the former site of the first colony) the pilot Fernandes ordered the colonists to disembark there instead of on the Chesapeake Bay area. As a privateer, he was anxious to attack Spanish shipping!

A relief expedition of 7 to 8 ships commanded by Sir Richard Grenville was scheduled to sail from England, but was overridden by order of the Privy Council because of the threat of the Spanish Armada in 1588. Only three years later in April, 1590 did another expedition arrive on the north end of Roanoke Island in the dark. No colonists remained in their village! They found "CRO" carved into a tree, and "CROATOAN" carved into a palisade.

REASONING OF THE PUZZLE

The colonists certainly couldn't have survived without the help of the Indians. Perhaps they joined the Indians as they moved to the island of Croatoan. Since that area wasn't rich in resources, about 1650 the Croatoan tribe finally settled at present Robertson County in the interior of what is now North Carolina. These Indians are known as the Hatteras or Lumnee Indians.

If the Indians had killed the colonists, their skeletons would have been left lying around. Indians didn't bury the bodies of their killed enemies.

These Indians have traditions that the Roanoke colonists joined with them. As evidence there are blue-eyed and yellow-haired individuals among the Indians, as well as knowledge of English words.

Hamilton MacMillan in 1880 proposed a creditable theory. He lived in Robeson County, southwestern North Carolina. Nearby there was a settlement of Pembroke Indians, who clamed their ancestors came from "Roanoke in Virginia". There Indians spoke pure Anglo-Saxon English, bore the last names of many of the lost colonists, and had European features (fair eyes, light-colored hair, and an Anglo-Saxon facial bone structure).

There is talk of doing an excavation of the village on Roanoke Island.

Better is a DNA examination of a sample of ten English-resembling Indians and ten standard-appearing Indians of the tribe, and ten of another N.C. tribe. If each DNA test cost $100, a minimum testing cost of $3,000 should easily be in the range of a college study (perhaps for earning doctorates). Perhaps useful markers might be found in the DNA.

Would a mixture of Indian and colonist blood inherit immunity to European diseases?

B. *Virginia Massacres*

Chief Powhatan died in 1618, succeeded by his brother Opitchapam, who was old and feeble. His other brother Opechancanough became the chief in reality. Opechancaough ordered the attack on the English settlements March 2, 1622 after meeting John Rolfe, who may have claimed Indian succession rights because he was Pocahontas' husband.

In the attack 347-400 (about one-third of the colonists) were killed, men, women, and children. Jamestown was saved by a warning of the attack from Richard Pace, the owner of a plantation three miles from Jamestown along the James River. A native servant ("Chanco") told him what the Indians intended. Unfortunately there wasn't time to notify the widely scattered plantations before the attack. The Indians mingled with the colonists without weapons, and then killed the colonists with whatever was at hand upon a signal. The Indians withdrew from the attack whenever they encountered resistance.

The colonists couldn't catch the Indians afterwards to punish them. They destroyed Indian fields and crops. May 22, 1623 William Tucker and another dozen colonists met with Chief Opechancanough to ratify the Chief's peace suggestions and to receive the English captives. The colony's physician John Pott poisoned the white wine in a cask that the Indians drank from. This killed about 200 Indians by poison, 50 more being killed by hand. The Chief was not harmed. This atrocity would not have been perpetuated by Captain John Smith (in England now) since it would have violated his mercenary's code.

Probably the colonists felt that this was "tit for tat"!

A second Indian attack occurred April 18, 1644. They killed 400-500 colonists (about one-sixth of the colonists), less relative damage than the first attack. Again no weapons were exhibited by the Indians before the attack. The furious colonists destroyed Powhatan's confederacy, with support of the English government because Virginia was made a royal colony of England in 1624. The 100-year old Indian Chief Opechancanough was bayoneted by one of his jailors after his capture two years after the attack.

Did the Indians use this "surprise attack" method earlier against Indian foes? This was intended for total extermination of the enemy. You can't accuse the Indian of cowardice since this was only a successful stratagem to them!

Chief Pontiac's assault on a British fort at Mackinaw in 1763 started with a large group of Ojibwas who approached the fort in friendly fashion and started a game of lacrosse beneath the walls of the fort. The British came out to watch, leaving the gate of the fort open. At a signal the Indians brought war axes from the robes of their women and rushed into the unarmed gate. The carnage was almost total. Whether or not the Indians got the idea from Virginia a century earlier, at least this stratagem suited the Indian zeal for unanticipated attacks!

C. Indian Diplomacy

The Indian chiefs and sachems exhibited remarkable political maneu-vering ability against the English colonialists.

In the Jamestown, Virginia Colony the English arrived unsuspectingly in the middle of the powerful Powhatan Confederacy of Chief Powhatan. He had inherited six tribes from his father, and conquered at least twenty-two more. He tightly ran a martially adept empire. He collected 80% tributes from the conquered tribes, this tribute doing directly into his storehouses and temples. When he judged the time right, his warriors executed his orders with precision and without pity.

While he could have easily wiped out the early colony, he saw a use for the English if he could win them over as allies against hostile neighbor-ing tribes:

- Massawomecks (an Iroquois tribe to the north)
- Monacans (Sioux tribe to the west)
- Mannahoacs (")

In the Plymouth Colony in New England, the sachem (Massasoit) of the Pokanokets was in a difficult situation because of disease deaths. It was a virgin soil epidemic, a contagious against which his people had no resis-tance. It was probably bubonic plague gotten from European fishermen in modern Maine during 1619 through 1621. In some cases as much as 90% of the natives were killed. His warriors had diminished from 3000 to a few hundred. The Narragansetts, his main enemy, had 5000 fighting men who had not been affected by the plague. Massasoit attempted to use his alliance with other tribes (Massachusetts and Nausets) to neu-tralize the threat of the Narragansetts.

He decided to "make friendship" with the English. Squanto, the Indians' interpreter, was playing a "double game", trying to undermine Massasoit. Squanto died of either Indian fever or of poison!

The second generation of the English settlers wasn't really interested with cooperating with the Indians. They wanted to get the Indians' lands, regarding the Indians as an obstacle. This attitude lead to "King Phillips War", covered in another separate story.

It is as if these Indian chiefs and sachems had read Machiavelli!

D. *Princess Mataoka (Pocahontas)*

Millions of American men
Are in love with the
Daughter of Chief Powhatan,
Who was called "Pocahontas".

Her private Indian name was
"Matoaka", meaning "Little wanton";
When she became a Christian
Her baptized name was "Rebecca".

She interceded with her Father
To save Captain John Smith
From Indian execution; she was
The favorite of Chief Powhatan.

She was eleven years old at the time,
So she and Smith had no romance;
But she saved him and the Jamestown
Colony from Indian threats.

One night she came secretly
To warn Smith of a trap
Intended to kill him
At the risk of her life.

Later he was injured by the
Gunpowder bags on him
Exploding, causing such injuries
That he had to return to England.

She was told by the
Colonists that Smith had died;

She was kidnapped by the colonists
To use as a hostage against Powhatan.

John Rolfe was the colonist
Who developed Jamestown's
"Cash crop" of tobacco,
Becoming a well-to-do planter.

He became enamored of
Pocahontas, and sought
Permission from English
Authorities to marry her.

Powatan gave his consent to
The marriage, and afterwards
Was friendlier to the
English colonists.

They had a son Thomas;
Then they moved to live
In England, about 70 miles
Southwest of London.

Pocahontas became sick,
Probably caused by the
Coal-burning fumes in London
And surrounding areas.

She died in 1617 in England,
Saying: "At least the child survives".
She's buried in Gravesend,
A Princess in a foreign land!

Rolfe returned to Jamestown,
Leaving his ill son in England
To be raised and educated
By his brother Henry.

The Indian Massacre of the
Colonists occurred in 1622;
Rolfe was found dead
In an open field.

In 1640 the son of John Rolfe and
Pocahontas came to Jamestown
To receive a large inheritance of land
On the James River from Chief Powhatan.

Development of the land
Made him a rich plantation owner;
He married Jane Polythress, having
An important line of descendants.

Pocahontas was a Princess in Virginia,
And was treated as such when introduced
To the King and Queen of England;
She also saved Smith's life several times.

In saving Smith's life
She was saving the colony;
An encounter between colonists
And Indians that was fruitful!

E. Mrs. John Rolfe (Also Matoaka or Pocahontas or Rebecca)

Pocahontas, a daughter of Chief Powhatan on Virginia, was born about 1595. Her Indian name was Matoaka, but she was called "Pocahontas", which means "Little Wanton". She was a favorite of her father.

Captain John Smith was captured by the Indians in December, 1609. The Indians with him were tied to poles, tortured by the women, and disemboweled. Then Smith was brought to Chief Powhatan for judgment. As he was about to be clubbed to death, she threw herself upon him and pleaded with her father for Smith's life, which he granted. It is not certain whether or not this was a planned charade. Since she had not met Smith before and was only ten years old, these two could not have had any romantic interests. But she did exhibit a special sympathy for Smith and the other English colonialists.

In January, 1609 she went to Smith and told him that her father intended to kill him and his men. Some Indians were going to bring him a banquet, and, while they ate, the Indians were going to kill him and his men. She said that her life would be forfeit if her father learned that she had warned him! Forewarned, Smith was able to thwart the planned massacre. This was the second, time she had saved Smith's life?!

In October, 1609 Smith was badly injured by a gunpowder explosion, having to return to England. It is undetermined whether this really was an "accident". Pocahontas was told that he had died. After Smith left the colony, she was kidnapped by the colonialists as hostage for a ransom from Chief Powhatan. She was converted to Christianity and baptized in 1614 as "Rebecca".

In April, 1614 she married John Rolfe of the Virginia colony. The wedding had the approval of English authorities and of Chief Powhatan. As long as she lived, the Chief was very friendly with the colonialists. They had one child, Thomas, in the marriage.

They arrived in Plymouth, England in June, 1616 to live with an entourage of ten or twelve male Powhatan Indians.

In England she was introduced as a princess to Queen Anne by Lady Delaware. She was frequently admitted to wait on her majesty. In England Pocahontas was treated like a princess, which she really was! She met James I at a royal Twelfth Night Masque in Whitehall Palace in 1617. In 1617 Smith called upon her in England. She hadn't seen him for eight years, and the encounter was strained. They never met again. The Rolfe's' lived about seventy miles from London. She was adversely affected by the black sooty smoke from the extensive coal burning in London. She died in March, 1617 from pneumonia or tuberculosis, and is buried in Gravesend, England.

Her widower returned to Jamestown. He couldn't safely take his ailing son Thomas. Thomas was left to the care of Rolfe's brother. Thomas went to Virginia in 1640 to receive his extensive inheritance of land on the James River from his grandfather Chief Powhatan. Development of this land made Thomas wealthy. He married Jane Polythress, having a daughter, Jane Rolfe. Later generations of the Virginia aristocracy trace their bloodlines back to Pocahontas' son.

Millions of American men have fallen in love with Pocahontas!

F. Indians Fight Colonists: A Free-for-all in New England

In 1675-76 in New England occurred "King Phillip's War", a devastating war between the Colonists and the Indians.

The new sachem of the Pokanoket in 1657 was Alexander. In 1662 the Plymouth Court ordered him to Plymouth in an arrogant attempt to exert control. Alexander died after questioning, angering his successor Phillip and the other Pokanokets. Phillip was convinced that his brother was poisoned by the English.

John Sassamon (a "praying Indian") was the son-in-law of Philip's sister Annie. In January of 1675 he told Joseph Winslow that Phillip was on the edge of war. Not long afterwards Sassamon died on the ice. An Indian claimed that Tobias (one of Phillip's senior counselors), Tobias's son, and one other killed Sassamon. A miscarriage of judgment occurred with the jury finding all the defendants guilty and executed. Phillip now had to wage war or lose his status as sachem of the Indians.

Phillip started selling land for muskets, since all his tribe's weapons had been seized by the Plymouth government. Since his tribe was only 5% of the Indians, he sought allies with the Pocassets, the Nemaaskets, and the Nipmucks. Once the fighting started, Phillip moved his warriors out of Plymouth Bay by canoe, ensuring a wider war.

The colonists in their war hysteria treated even friendly Indians as hostile, getting Philip Indian allies who would otherwise have remained neutral, such as the Narragansetts.

Fortunately for the Colonists the Mohawks (and the Iroquois League) remained allies of the English! The fighting was savage and destructive to both sides.

Killing Phillip in 1676 stopped this war but not the hostilities. The Colonists sent all Indians who fought for Phillip as slaves to Caribbean plantations, virtually a death sentence. The English had reduced their belt of friendly Indians surrounding them, which considerably protected the Colonists against Indian attacks. For the next century there were many destructive Indian attacks in New England.

G. Stealing Indian Lands

This subject matter has a really big scope. The Author only illustrates several historical examples, with the certainty there are many more examples.

General Oglethorpe of England was the founder of the Colony of Georgia. He made the first English treaty with the Creek Indians. White men moved into the territory, built rough log cabins, and staked unauthorized claims on Indian lands.

When he returned to England, William Stephens, President of the Georgia Trustees, took over. He made new agreements, taking more land, subsequently breaking every agreement made. He used the Georgia Militia to enforce move of the Indians further west. Government agents bribed and lied to the Cherokee leaders for the Indian lands.

Government land grants were given to white settlement from 1790 onward. The state governor declared war on the Cherokee nations, forcing them to sell all their Georgia lands. Whites no longer had to honor contracts or agreements made with the Indians.

The Indian lands in western Georgia were seized by the Indian Treaty of 1825, which wasn't ratified by the government. In 1827 Georgia held a Land Lottery by which Indian lands were granted to white settlers before the U.S. Government agreed to pay the Indians for their lands. In 1830 Congress passed the Indian Removal Act.

The War Department appointed "the reverend John F. Schernerhorn" as a special commissioner to get the Cherokees to voluntarily agree to the government plans. He lied and cheated. In 1827 the U.S. Government allowed officially the Indians two years to give their homeland to border settlers who were already invoking the treaty. In 1838 the "Trail of Tears" exodus of the Indians to Oklahoma was started.

In 1823 the Supreme Court issued a decision that the Indians could occupy lands within the U.S. but couldn't hold title to those lands! The Indians' "right of occupancy" was subordinate to the United States' "right of discovery". Of course, the Indians had discovered these lands hundreds of years before the white settlers arrived!

In 1831 the Cherokees based an appeal on a Georgia law which prohibited whites from living on Indian Territory after March 31, 1831, without a license from the state. The court decided in favor of the Cherokees, but the state of Georgia refused to abide by the Court decision and President Jackson refused to enforce the law.

Out west white settlers used violence to drive off the Indians and seize their lands. Perhaps they didn't have any lawyers!

All this is like the chicken being tried by a jury of foxes! (Uncle Remus)

H. Pontiac's Uprising

A. Preamble to War

The British won the "French and Indian War", getting control of the French assets in the North American continent. The Indians were used to the French being friendly, giving them gifts, and trading for furs. The British had a very strict regulation of the fur trade.

British General Amherst, commander in chief of His Majesty's forces in North America, controlled the British military forces in the Lakes region and in the "Ohio Country". He didn't believe in giving gifts to the Indians, considering that to be "bribery". He also looked down on the Indian as "savages". The General also ordered the forts to keep the Indians short of ammunition and powder. This was a hardship for the Indians because they had grown dependent on hunting with guns instead of with bows and arrows, becoming dependent on colonists' goods. He also issued an edict prohibiting the sale of rum to Indians.

The French wanted to trade with the Indians, not take their lands. The English Colonists, on the other hand, felt that the "French and Indian war" was fought so the Colonists could settle in the Indian lands, especially in the "Ohio Country". George Washington was only one of the colonist "land speculators"!

B. The Indian Uprising in 1763

In 1763 Chief Pontiac (Indian name was Obwandigyag) of the Ottawas organized a plan for several Indian tribes to attack Fort Detroit. Other Indian tribes were passing around "war belts", setting up other aggressive actions against the British and the colonists. Many of the Indians had fought for the French in the "French and Indian war".

Pontiac's attack plan involved infiltrating his Indian warriors into Fort Detroit, and them attacking on a signal. He and 300 of his warriors entered the fort and asked to talk with Major Gladwin. The Indians had weapons concealed in their blankets. Ottawa men and women quietly spread around the inside of the fort. He didn't give the signal because the garrison was "on alert". Someone had betrayed him, but other forts were taken by surprise attacks. Usually the fort garrisons were killed, but the French settlers saved some of them. Both Fort Detroit and Fort Pitt withstood the Indian attacks. The Indians did sieges of them.

A famous example of a successful Indian ruse was at Fort Michilimackinac, one of the largest and most important of the interior French forts. The Indians distracted the garrison with a game of lacrosse by following a stray ball into the open gate of the fort.

In 1763 the British in two months lost every fort in the Lakes and Ohio Country except Fort Detroit and Fort Pitt. 2500 whites were killed. General Amherst was so furious with the Indians that he approved a plan to infect the Indians with smallpox-contaminated blankets!

The Battle of Devil's Hole (fall, 1763) was the Colonists costliest defeat of the war in terms of men killed. The battle was at the north end of the Niagara Portage about three miles from Fort Schlosser.

The Battle of Bushy Run August 5-6 is considered by many historians as the greatest military victory ever in frontier warfare. British Colonel Henry Bouquet used a feigned retreat to become the victor over a substantially larger Indian force. This broke the back of the revolt.

Pontiac only commanded as long as his followers believed in him. The followers weren't obligated to follow orders they didn't believe in. His alliance began to disintegrate. After the final peace in July 23-25, 1765, Chief Pontiac became an important regional figure. He had the understanding that the British didn't own the land, but only rented it.

C. Aftermath of the War

Chief Pontiac advocated a return to the days of French control of the region. The colonists still wanted the Indian lands, this being one of the areas on contention between the British and the Colonists leading to the American War of Independence.

He was murdered by a Peoria Indian at Cahokia, perhaps in retaliation for his stabbing Chief Makatahinga (Blue Dog) in an altercation at Detroit. He set afire the "Ohio Country" against the British. In the early 1800's Chief Tecumseh of the Shawnees set it afire again with alliance with the British against the Colonists.

The American Colonists and their state legislatures were reluctant to support the British in their campaigns with either fighting men fighting outside their state, and/or with money and supplies. The British hiked taxes on the Colonists to meet the British needs, further infuriating the Colonists.

D. Scorecard of General Amherst

Activity	Plus	Minus
1. Haughty towards the Indians		X
2. No gifts to Indians		X
3. Keep Indians short of ammunition and powder		X
4. Prohibited sale of rum to the Indians	0.5	0.5
5. Spread smallpox to Indians		X
6. Reinforced Fort Detroit		X
7. Reinforced Fort Pitt		X
8. Developed a strategy to defeat the Indians		X

He ranks high as a General fighting a war, but low as a diplomat! He was not blamed for the war, being strongly supported by British Prime Minister William Pitt, who was one of the prime architects of the war in America. When finally relieved to return to England, he continued to serve. He wound up as a field marshal, the highest rank in the British Army.

Just resuming gifts to the Indians wouldn't have solved the problem of the Colonists settling Indian lands.

I. *Tecumseh's Indian Confederacy*

Tecumseh was born in 1768 in the "Ohio Country". He was named for a "Shooting Star" and became one of the Shawnee's greatest leaders. He was trained by Chiksika to become a warrior. He fought against the English from 1782 on. He was an excellent orator and organizer, open and honest, and a strong, respected war chief by 1808. He attracted many of the younger, more anti-American warriors.

He didn't believe in killing women and children in war. He refused to torture prisoners. Part of the Shawnee tradition was to adopt defeated enemies into the tribe. He also had a distinguished appearance.

The Treaty of Greeneville in 1795 had the Indians give up all their land except the northwestern corner of present-day Ohio. Tecumseh was one of the Indians who disagreed with their tribes' actions, and refused to sign the treaty.

By the early 1800's he decided that the only way to stop white advancement was to form a confederacy of Indian tribes west of the Appalachian Mountains. He believed that no single tribe owned the land, and that only all tribes together could turn land over to the whites. He believed that the Indians only had a chance militarily against the Americans if the

Indians united. This had been advocated earlier by the Shawnee leader Blue Jacket and the Mohawk leader Joseph Brant.

Tecumseh's younger brother, Tenskwatawa, the Prophet, helped Tecumseh unite the Indians. The Prophet had a vision that the Master of Life (the Shawnees' primary god) told him to have the Indians give up all white customs and products.

In 1808 the two brothers set up a new town at Prophetsville at the intersection of the Tippecanoe and Wabash rivers, 75 miles south of Lake Michigan, and 50 miles north of Fort Harrison. Tecumseh was repelled by the fanaticism in many of the Prophet's followers.

In 1811 the governor of the Indiana Territory, William Henry Harrison., led an army towards the village. Against Tecumseh's orders (and in his absence traveling south to persuade the southeastern tribes to join his confederacy) the Prophet sent his warriors against the Americans. In this "Battle of Tippecanoe" the Americans won and destroyed Prophetsville. This victory eventually resulted in Harrison becoming a U.S. President.

This victory tremendously weakened Tecumseh's Confederation.

During the War of 1812 Tecumseh and his remaining followers allied themselves with the British. Tecumsah died at the Battle of the Thames. A combined English-Indian force met an American army led by William Henry Harrison. The British broke and ran from the battlefield. The Indians were driven from the field.

Tecumseh was killed in battle in the woods by Richard Johnson. His death signified the end of united Indian resistance against the Americans.

The Confederacy

While most tribes listened to his proposals, many rejected his ideas. Especially the Indians in present-day Tennessee, Georgia, and Mississippi embraced white products and customs. He had more success in Ohio,

Kentucky, and the Indiana territory, areas that the whites had been attempting to settle since before the French and Indian War.

As his followers converged at Prophetstown, he couldn't supply them with firearms and ammunition. To acquire white goods, the Indians engaged in the fur trade with the Americans.

He traveled down the "Six Towns' Trail" into east-central Mississippi. He reached Mokolube, the principle Choctaw town near modern day Philadelphia. He tried to recruit followers, but he was shadowed by Choctaw Chief Pushmataha, who urged the Indians to remain friendly toward the United States. The Choctaws generally rejected Tecumseh's overtures. Chief Pushmataha was later invited to Washington, D. C., where he died of a surfeit of drink and food supplied by his hosts (the U.S. government).

Tecumseh went next to the Creeks, his mother's tribe. Many young Creeks were interested in his message. This precipitated strife among the Creeks by Tecumseh's followers, leading to the Creek Uprising of 1813. Andrew Jackson defeated the Creeks at the Battle of Horseshoe Bend in 1813.

The Final Outcome

Which is better: war or submission?

The Shawnees chose to fight the whites in the "Ohio Country". They were shattered in battle with white armies.

The Choctaws in Alabama and Mississippi chose to submit, selling their lands and being moved to settlements in Oklahoma. In walking to the reservations many died, especially the old and children. They were treated poorly in the reservations.

Which choice would you make, knowing there is no "good" outcome for you?! The Indians in North and South America who died from European diseases didn't get these choices

J. Removal of the Cherokees to West of the Mississippi

The Indian Removal Act of 1830

President Andrew Jackson felt strongly that the Indians should be moved west of The Mississippi so contact with whites would be broken. And, of course, the whites would gain control of the Indian lands east of the Mississippi with minimal or no compensation to the Indians.

President Jackson pushed the "Indian Removal Act" through the U.S. Senate. President Jackson promptly signed the bill into law. The Cherokees established an independent Cherokee Nation. In 1832 the U.S. Supreme Court ruled in favor of the Cherokees. Chief Justice John Marshall ruled that the Cherokee Nation was sovereign, making the removal laws invalid. The Cherokee would have to agree to removal in a treaty, with the treaty being ratified by the U.S. Senate.

A minority (less than 500 out of the 17,000 Cherokee in North Georgia) signed the Treaty of New Ochota, signed by Major Ridge and members of the Treaty Party. The treaty passed the Senate by a single vote. This gave President Jackson the legal document to remove the Indians. In 1838 the U.S. began the removal to Oklahoma.

The Cherokee "Trail of Tears"

In 1828 gold was discovered in the North Georgia Mountains. The gold rush of 1829 brought thousands of people into the Cherokee Nation. This increased the pressure in Georgia to move the Cherokees to West of the Mississippi River.

In 1837 the U.S. Government allowed the Indians two years officially to resettle. General John Wood resigned his command in protest. General Winfield Scott arrived at New Ochota on May 17, 1838 with 7000 soldiers to start the process of removal of an estimated 16,000 Cherokees. The Cherokee men, women, and children were herded into makeshift forts with minimal facilities and food, and then forced to march a thousand miles to Oklahoma, at the average of ten miles per day. The human losses of the first groups were very high, especially among the children and the old.

John Ross appealed to General Scott to let his people lead the tribe west. After Scott agreed, Ross organized the Cherokee into smaller groups, and let them move separately through the wilderness foraging for food. This significantly reduced the loss of life.

About 4000 Cherokee died as a result of the removal along the trail known as the "Trail of Tears". The U.S. Government's fault was in not being watchful of those taken into their charge.

The Cherokee killed Major Ridge, his son, and Elias Boudinot for signing the Treaty of New Ochota. More than 200 Indians escaped into the mountains of Georgia and the eastern part of Tennessee. This and other things clearly indicated that the Cherokee weren't moving voluntarily!

An example is a group of 2000 (as a division) being moved in 1839. There were about ten officers and overseers in each detachment to provide supplies for the journey and to attend to the general wants of the company As the Indians came in, they were furnished rations by lodges, each lodge to receive corn, oats, and fodder. The hunters supplied meat out of the woods. Each morning when the Indians broke camp they were told how far they had to go and in which direction. At each allowed stop the dead (often fourteen or fifteen) were buried. Many escaped during the marches.

In Oklahoma the young were sent to "boarding schools" where they were "civilized" by being given white names, allowed to speak only English, and forbidden to worship their "pagan gods".

Perhaps the "theft" of the Indian lands was inevitable, but the Indian removals were not done well.

K. Why did the Indians lose to the white Armies in the long run?

(1) The Indians couldn't keep their warriors in the field year round. They had to hunt for their villages. Their winter stocks were usually only enough for winter. In Spring the warriors had to intensively hunt game and the women plant crops (especially corn).

(2) The white armies couldn't finish off Indians in the field, but their villages were a more stationary target. In Virginia the whites destroyed Powhatan's villages' crops and stores. The American Army couldn't catch Geronimo and his Apache warriors. But, with the help of other Apache tribe trackers, they could follow them to their villages, or reservations, and attack them there. Even in Mexico! One Apache tribe didn't feel unity with another tribe.

(3) In the open warfare of the West, the Indians couldn't counter the white's cannon and gatling guns (during and after the Civil War).

IV. The American Revolution

A. On the Road to Revolution

The French and Indian War was the local American name for a world-wide war between England and France, called the Seven Years War in Europe. The war started in North America in 1754 (ostensibly started by a 22-year old militia Major George Washington), spreading to Europe only in 1756. The war ended with the Treaty of Paris in 1763 which turned over everything in North America east of the Mississippi River to the English, except New Orleans, which went to the Spanish along with French claims of lands west of the Mississippi.

This treaty confirmed England's commercial supremacy and cemented control of the settled regions of North Carolina.

However, precedents and entanglements were set up leading considerable strain between the American colonists and England:

(1) The colonists learned that they would have to fight for their lives and lands, especially against the Indians; The colonists got real combat experience that paid off in the Revolution.

(2) The war was very costly for England. To build up England governmental resources more taxes had to be raised from the colonists, notably the Stamp tax. Also more control must be exerted over the colonists, such as prohibiting manufacture in North American competing with English merchants and shippers. This particularly annoyed the colonists who considered themselves as good as Englishmen.

(3) The English authorities prohibited the colonists from going into the Ohio Country. The colonists thought that one of the main purposes of the war against the French was to enable such colonization. European settlements that violated the 1963 Proclamation were burned by royal troops.

(4) During the war the colonists resisted efforts by the English government to force equipment, shelter, and manpower from the colonists.

(5) English troops were permanently quartered in the colonies.

Starting from these resentments among the colonists and add a few incidents following from the resentments and you can readily see how the Revolution happened:

(1) The "Boston Massacre" in 1770 where British soldiers killed five colonists.

(2) Actions against the hated "Stamp Taxes" was exhibited in the tea dumped in Boston harbor (Boston Tea Party of 1773), as well as other incidents.

(3) The first of the Intolerable Acts was passed by Parliament as punishment for the Boston Tea Party;

(4) In 1775 gunfire exchanged between British soldiers and colonists between Lexington and Concord;

(5) In 1776 Norfolk, Virginia was burned by Lord Dunmore;

(6) Rhode Islanders did a lot of smuggling, risky trading (such as salves), and other "shady" transactions.

The English felt justified in their actions against the colonists. The colonists resented the English efforts to "control" and tax them. Force of arms was ultimately resolved for the colonists because of the French government's support. Perhaps this was the French revenge for their losses in the French and Indian War!

I had never really thought about the precursors of the American Revolution until I saw the PBS Home Video production of: "The War That Made America". It certainly convinced me that one war led to the next one!

B. French Support of the American Revolution

Benjamin Franklin was the Colonists' first Ambassador to France in 1776.

There is little doubt that, without Franklin's dedicated service in France, the colonists would have lost the war with England:

- he obtained multiple loans to finance American troops fighting the British, with very lenient terms
- he negotiated and signed a Treaty of Alliance between France and the United States
- in 1776 he left for the Minister of Foreign Affairs, Count de Vergennes, a sketch to apply for 8 ships of the line (manned), 20 to 30,000
- muskets and bayonets, and large quantities of armaments and brass field pieces to be sent under convoy.
- he was instrumental in sending the Marquis de Lafayette to train American troops in 1778
- in 1783 he signed the Treaty of Paris, which ended the war with England

After Burgoyne's surrender at Saratoga in 1777 of one-fourth the British forces in North America., the French were sure that the Revolution would succeed. The Colonists were proven effective in battle against the British army.

The French wanted revenge against the British for the loss of Canada in the Seven Years War.

We could not have achieved our independence from Britain without the French help. This is very evident in the decisive Battle of Yorktown!

C. Saratoga: The Turning Point of the American Revolution

General Burgoyne arrived in Quebec on May 6, 1777. He planned to leave Canada, traverse Lake Champlain, and march with his 8000 troops and cannon to a pivotal battle in Albany, New York. General Howe and Clinton (the Governor of New York) were to cooperate with him, giving Burgoyne support, especially needed because of Burgoyne's long supply line to Canada.

General Howe and Governor Clinton didn't keep in touch with Burgoyne, and didn't give him any effective help, either of troops or supplies. Historian Richard M. Ketchum in "Saratoga: Turning Point of America's Revolution" reaches the conclusion that Burgoyne's campaign was intended as a diversionary campaign without Burgoyne knowing this!

The Fighting

As Burgoyne fought his way down the Hudson River he encountered large numbers of American soldiers. His destination of Albany, New York wasn't a secret from the Americans. He kept losing Indians who he depended for reconnaissance. The Indians quickly lost belief in the success of this project, meaning no loot for them. Burgoyne really didn't know where his American enemy was much of the time.

At Bemis Heights he cut off his Canadian supply line, intending to fight a pivotal battle at Albany.

At Freeman Farm (just north of Bemis Heights) Burgoyne lost eight cannon and more than 400 officers and men. With aggressive attacks by American General Arnold, the British were losing. Probably only darkness saved Burgoyne from immediate disaster. At night on October 8 the British began their retreat to the heights of Saratoga.

The British were short of food and fodder for their horses.

The battles were unusually fierce, the Americans showing better resolution than before.

Surrender at Saratoga

On October 12, 1777 General Burgoyne decided to retreat, leaving their artillery and baggage behind. That night Baron Riedesel was told, at 10 PM, that the retreat that night was postponed, no reason given.

By the next morning the British were surrounded by superior numbers of American troops with cannon. Burgoyne could no longer retreat and had to surrender on October 17 with his 3500 effective combatants and cannon.

At first Burgoyne was given liberal surrender terms. Congress thought the actual surrender terms were too lenient and changed them. Burgoyne and some of his officers were allowed to return to England, but the rest of his troops were held in Virginia as prisoners until the end of the war. This broke the American word at the surrender.

Within two days after the surrender (formal treaty signed February 6, 1778):

(1) The King of France signed a short note virtually making France an ally of the U.S.;

(2) The British ambassador to France left for London, and France and England were at war;

(3) The Americans captured seven generals with their staffs, 678 other officers, 197 Musicians, 4,836 private soldiers, 27 cannon, 5000 stand of small arms, much ammunition, and military stores and equipment;

(4) After a considerable delay, Spain and Holland came into the conflict on the American side.

The effects of this American victory made the success of the American Revolution possible, especially because of the support of the French fleet and army, and increased aid.

D. Yorktown: the French and the Colonials Defeat the British

By 1781 the Revolutionary War had been going since 1775 and both the British and Colonial public were tired of it. Britain's fleet could land soldiers anywhere in the colonies. The British were doing a Southern military push. While the northern colonies had 2 out of 3 colonists supporting revolution, in the South the Loyalists were 1 out of every 2 colonists.

In 1779 Sir Henry Clinton in New York was Commander-in-chief of all Her Majesty's forces in America. He organized a large-scale raid of Virginia. He intended Lord Cornwallis to make the security of South Carolina his main object. After the destruction of Gates' army in 1780 at the Battle of Camden, Cornwallis had undisputed possession of the Carolinas.

Cornwallis was convinced that the conquest of Virginia would be followed by control of all the colonies. He marched his forces from Petersburg in May 24th.

Washington wrote to General Lafayette to dispose his troops so as to prevent Cornwallis from retiring to North Carolina. Lafayette moved his division to a position near Williamsburg in Cornwallis' rear.

Lieutenant General de Rochambeau (in control of the French army) and Admiral Deschambault agreed to send all the French forces to operate with Lafayette against General Arnold (now a British general). In august, 1781 the decision was made to conduct a strategic march against the English Army in Virginia.

The French fleet had sailed from France to the West Indies, and there to the Chesapeake area, arriving before the British fleet sailing to help Cornwallis. In September, 1781 the British fleet was turned away by battle. Comte de Grasse' 24 French ships of the line drove off 19 British ships under Admiral Graves in early September, 1781.

The French fleet landed French soldiers and artillery. Washington had 11,000 men under Lafayette fighting in the battle while the French had at least 29,000 soldiers and sailors. These French military resources and the French fleet played a critical role in trapping the 8,700 strong British army and winning the engagement.

E. Justice for Arnold

In ancient Rome strict discipline was maintained in the army. In a particular legion, two soldiers had a homosexual attachment. In battle one of the pair fell down and the other soldier broke ranks to help him. After the battle the second soldier was given an award for fighting valiantly. Then he was executed for breaking ranks. **This was Roman justice!**

General Benedict Arnold was a brave, successful General in the first part of the Revolutionary War against the British. He was a superb battlefield soldier, with the ability to command his troops to extend themselves in battle. He was a hero until he plotted with the British to deliver West Point to them. If this had succeeded, the upper part of New York State would have been open to the British and Tories (American loyalists). He might actually have changed the course of the war!

The plot failed, with Major Andre being hanged by our side. General Arnold was able to get to an English ship. He was made a Major General in the British Army. He was not as successful as a "Headquarters General" as he had been in battle. The British took him back with them to England when the War was over.

The author's psychological analysis of Arnold:

General Gates, his superior, was jealous of him. Arnold was given no role in the Battle of Saratoga, but he showed up anyway! He went on the field and rallied soldiers into aggressive attacks which made the difference in helping the colonists win the battle. He was severely wounded in his right leg, but he wouldn't let the surgeons amputate. After this he couldn't participate in a battle on horse, and was given the token role of command of the West Point Armory. He married a women whose father was an ardent loyalist. Given his vanity, it was probably easy for the British to "turn him", promising him promotion as a British General.

If Arnold had died at Saratoga, he would be remembered today as a great American hero!

It is too bad that General Arnold couldn't have been given "**American Justice**"!

F. Loyalists

The Loyalists (also called Tories) were those colonists (perhaps 16%) who didn't want to break away from Britain. Quite a few were part of the British Forces that fought to hold onto their territories in North America. The wealthiest and most influential people were Loyalists, as were many small farmers and tradesmen. The Loyalists tended to be foreign-born and of the Anglican religion.

Loyalists were probably a majority in New York, New Jersey, Georgia, and the Carolinas. They were weakest in the old colonies, Virginia and Massachusetts. There is mention of "unfriendly Quakers" as Loyalists in Pennsylvania. The German and Dutch colonists tended to favor the royal government. The Scottish highlanders in South Carolina and Georgia made Tory strongholds.

The Johnsons strongly influenced the Indians to the Loyalist cause. This influence was backed by munificent gifts to the Indians of arms, clothing, and other desirables by Sir Guy Carleton on behalf of the British government. While the Oneida and Tuscarawas of the Six Nations decided not to take any part in the Revolution, the other four Indian nations continued to back the British government. The Iroquois League remembered the backing of the British forces for the past 100 years against the Algonquians.

Their opposition to independence or their willingness to support British solders led to intimidation and violence, such as tarring and feathering. Many state legislatures passed laws enabling the confiscation of Loyalist property.

Loyalist regiments were formed in several theatres and participated in some of the bitterest engagements of the war. Over 19,000 Loyalists served in specially created provincial corps, accompanied by several thousand Indians (including the Mohawks).

At the end of the war thousands of Loyalists found Canada a friendly destination, also the Bahamas, West Indies, and England. Many were given land grants, especially in the Niagara Peninsula which had very poor soil. Life was hard because supplies were delayed, food was scarce, and the extremely cold winter killed off their crops.

Many also settled in the Bay of Quinte area, where the lands had to be bought from the Mississauga Indians. The Loyalists needed support from the government to become self-sufficient.

Several thousand slaves fought on the Loyalist side, later migrating to Nova Scotia or to Sierra Leone in Africa.

The migration of 50,000 Loyalists to Canada made Canada bilingual, and brought new economic life to Canada. Between 80,000 and 100,000 eventually fled, almost half to Canada (the main wave in 1783-1784).

In determining who was eligible for compensation for war losses, Britain decided that Loyalists were those born or living in the American colonies at the outbreak of the Revolution who rendered substantial service to the royal cause during the war, and who left the US by the end of the war or soon after.

V. Colonial and U.S. History

A. British Privateers Against Spain

A "letter of marque" licensed "private men of war' to raid enemy sea commerce and take prizes. The costs of commissioning privateers were borne by investors, who divided the prizes. A crew under a "letter of marque" received regular wages in addition to returns from captures. Privateers brought their prizes to English ports (Bristol and Plymouth were quite popular). The Admiralty valued and sold the prizes, keeping 10% for the government, also charging port fees.

Technically a privateer was only entitled to attack enemy vessels during wartime. However, states often encouraged attacks on opposing powers while at peace, or on neutral vessels during time of war, blurring the line between privateering and piracy. If the Spanish had caught Sir Francis Drake, they would have treated him and his men as pirates! There was no real difference in the flags flown by royal and private ships before 1634.

English Queen Elizabeth I (the daughter of King Henry VIII and Queen Anne Boleyn) needed money badly for her governmental and personal finances. Also the use of privateers increased the ships available for action by England without additional cost expended by England.

The piracy and privateering forced the Spanish to institute the "convoy system" for the treasure ships coming from the Caribbean. Men-of-war accompanied and protected the treasure ships. In their fury the Spanish finally resorted to the Spanish Armada of 1688 against England, an attempt to conquer England and restore Catholicism. The English used their royal men-of-war and the privateer ships against them. The smaller English ships sailed rings around the larger, clumsily-handled Spanish ships! The Spanish fleet was turned away with the loss of three of their ships. A storm in the English Channel did the most damage to the Spanish, who arrived back in Spain with only one-quarter of their original fleet.

It is remarkable that the English didn't kill the Spanish seamen who swam ashore in Ireland. They were allowed to make their homes where they landed, becoming the famous "black Irish"!

Famous English privateers were Sir Francis Drake, Sir John Hawkins, Captain Christopher Newport, and Sir Henry Morgan, who sacked the city of Panama!

A lesser known privateer was the English explorer Bartholomew Gosnold, who discovered and named Cape Cod and Martha's Vinyard, and was the "prime mover" of the Jamestown, Virginia colony.

Some privateers went on to become pirates. Such was Edward Teach ("Blackbeard"), who was eventually tried as a pirate, convicted, and hanged.

The Stuart monarch (James I) after Elizabeth I forbade privateering. In 1856 the Declaration of Paris was signed by all major European powers. It stated: "Privateering is and remains abolished."

B. The Life of a Caribbean Pirate

Pirates have existed since men started using boats. An early incident was Mediterranean pirates capturing Julius Caesar (as a young man) and ransoming him. He told them that he'd hunt them down. He did!

Living Conditions

In the Caribbean the pirates could sleep on deck in warm weather. Since pirate ships were over-manned for use in boarding other ships or taking cities, the crews had lots of leisure time to play cards or dice, drink, and fire guns (if there was extra ammunition).

The diet was meat, leaving them vulnerable to scurvy.

Venereal diseases were common. They used mercury compounds for treatment of syphilis.

The Captain

There were no class distinctions on board and no one was set in authority over the Captain. He was selected for superior knowledge and boldness. A Captain could easily be deposed, only getting two shares of the booty.

In engagements he commanded absolute obedience. He could then shoot anyone not obeying his commands.

The Captain had to know about new colonies, new wars, new alliances and the general development of trade. He had to know the value of things so he could divide the booty. He dispensed justice. Pirates had to apply to him to fight with each other.

Articles were drawn up and sworn on a Bible or on an axe.

"Marooning" was seriously taken since few survived being put shore on a deserted island far from civilization.

Other Officers

The Sailing Master was responsible for the setting of sails and for the course once the Captain selected a destination. If a captured Sailing Master joined the pirates, he got a 1 ¾ share of the booty. Navigators were also in demand.

The Quartermaster was the "strong man" of the ship. His job was to enforce the Captain's orders. He was in charge of the selection and division of the booty. He got two shares of the booty money.

Capture

The British hanged pirates, while the Spanish preferred garroting. The pirates were hanged publicly, and usually allowed to rot until the rope rotted through.

Pirates from captured boats could be acquitted if they had been forced to join the pirates.

Many pirates considered a few years of freedom and independence to be worth the price of being hung when caught. The average age of a pirate in 1722 was 28. The life of a pirate appealed to the rebellious individualistic spirit of the English.

The Piracy Act of 1721 extended the penalties for piracy to anyone who traded with or exchanged with the outlaws.

Treatment of Captives

Often captives were killed to prevent them later identifying the pirates and testifying against them. Women were often raped before being killed. "Walking the plank' was only one method of killing. The daughter of Aaron Burr was captured off the coast of the Carolinas and forced to "walk the plank". Sometimes captives were ransomed, but this was more dangerous to the pirates.

Life in the Royal Navy

Sailors in the Royal Navy got weekly pay and grog. In comparison to the pirates, discipline was strict. Sailors were flogged for minor offenses, and could be placed on "bread and water" in the ship's brig. To raise a hand against any ship's officer, to mutiny or inspire to mutiny was death. Class distinctions were always there, and enforced.

There wasn't much, if any, idle time.

Often new sailors were seized by "press gangs" in British ports, or from ships from the Colonies in America.

The pirates found that displaying their colors would often get surrender by the ship threatened. Destroying the ships by gunfire was not in the pirates' interests. The Navy would get up close and fire their cannon into the opposing ship, a dangerous but effective tactic. It took disciplined gun crews to be effective.

In a way, privateers had the relaxed discipline of the pirates along with legality. Of course, if the Spanish captured a British privateer ship, they would treat its crew as pirates.

C. Witches Versus Rye Ergot

The Salem Witchcraft trials in 1692 featured thirty victims with symptoms of fits, hallucinations, sensations of being bitten, and a burning sensation in their fingers, lameness, and/or temporary lameness. They blamed witchcraft!

Since I don't believe in witchcraft (although I do believe in human evil), I was receptive to a physical explanation. I saw an episode of NOVA on TV in which "rye ergot" was considered as the cause of the illness. Linda Caporael printed her research in "Ergotism: The Satan loosed in Salem?", Science, 1976.

Ergot is a fungus blight that forms hallucinogenic drugs in bread. The victims can appear bewitched, suffer paranoia and hallucinations, twitches and spasms, cardiovascular trouble, stillborn children, and weakens the immune system, like the symptoms seen in Salem. Did they have convulsive ergotism as opposed to gangrenous ergotism?

Ergot thrives in a cold winter followed by a wet spring. Rye was grown in Essex County when wheat crops were devastated by rust. The season had been warm and the growing area was swampy, an ideal environment for the development of ergot of rye.

Ergotism was never common in England because rye was little grown. Also, dairy products reduce convulsive ergotism. England's relative freedom from it was attributable to its diet rich in milk, butter, and cheese.

During the Middle Ages, tens of thousands of Europeans were afflicted by ergotism, with gangrenous extremities, convulsions, madness, and death. Denis Dodart reported the relationship between ergotized rye and bread poisoning in a letter to the French Royal Academie in 1676.

D. FIGHTING WHILE NEGOTIATING (1814)

By 1814 Britain had defeated Napoleon and could send more than 100 ships to extend its blockade over the entire Atlantic coast of North America. For months before the British fleet was due to arrive in force, Rear Admiral Sir George Cochrane had been raiding along the Eastern seaboard with ruthlessness.

The British did not intend to reconquer the United States, but rather to interfere with the American territorial land expansion. The areas of attack were:

- On August 16, 1814 more than 20 British ships entered the Chesapeake carrying several thousand land soldiers, half the fleet sailing up the Potomac, half towards Baltimore. Washington City was not defended well and the British took it, did a lot of damage, including burning the While House, then withdrawing to attack Baltimore, where Fort McHenry held, nullifying the attack.

- Land 3000–15,000 troops in Montreal to take control of the region around Lake Ontario. The British intended to destroy America's fleet on Lake Erie and then defeat Harrison on the ground. By separating western land from the eastern seaboard, Britain might again establish a New World colony. Perry's sea forces won.

- George Prevost was to sweep down from Canada to invade New York In August, 1814 Prevost's army was the largest and most lethal force (30,000 veteran troops). Britain had ever sent to North America. He was driving towards Albany, New York, but he depended on controlling Lake Champlain. A sea battle at Plattsburgh was won by America's Macdonough, forcing Prevost to retreat to the town of Champlain.

-In the South Sir Edward Pakenham would capture New Orleans. General Jackson arrived in New Orleans December 1, 1814 and took command of the American forces. With his knowledgeable and determined leadership the British had to retreat. Helping Jackson was the enlisting of Pirate Jean Lafitte and his forces, and the allowing of 500 blacks to fight on the American side

Meanwhile in Ghent there was held a peace conference between the United States and Britain in 1814 while the British were making their biggest military effort against America. The British diplomatic effort was based on probable military success (if any).

The British brought up new, surprising demands:

-create a vast neutral zone of Indian territory around the Great Lakes (designed to stop the western expansion of America, and gain influence with the Indians).

-Wanted to reverse Oliver Perry's victory by having the United States abandon its military positions around the Great Lakes.

-Calling for the United States to cede without compensation a portion of Maine to allow Britain to run a road from Halifax to Quebec.

It is interesting that the United States didn't bring up the British "pressing" America sailors. The U.S. delegation felt that peace would see an end to the main issue which caused the United States to declare war on Britain.

With the failure of the British effort against New Orleans, the British withdrew their excessive demands, and agreement was readily reached, allowing American fishermen to fish off Newfoundland. In 1815 the peace was finally agreed upon.

If the British military efforts had succeeded, their negotiating would have gone well for them, as well as retarding the territorial growth of the United States. This coordinated diplomatic-military effort shows what a great imperial power Britain was!

E. Will the Real Aaron Burr Please Stand Up!

Aaron Burr was so vilified by his political opponents (especially Alexander Hamilton) that his image in the history books is negative. What was the truth?

Alexander Hamilton, a long-term political foe, was always attacking Burr:

(1) Burr was devoid of principles-Actually Burr had a Utilitarian philosophy with an early affinity for anti-Federalism.

(2) Burr was privately reckless—He was only one of many politicians who speculated (including Washington and Hamilton).

(3) Burr was personally powerful

-The Author stipulates that Burr was intelligent, ambitious, and personable, but this was true of Hamilton also).

Burr's ambition showed up in his successful military career. He was aide to General Putnam in the invasion of Canada. In 1777 General Washington notified him of his promotion to Lieutenant General of the Continental Army. He found military solutions quickly, and developed organizational skills.

He devoted the 1780's to law practice. He was a very effective lawyer in the courtroom, impressively defending himself (successfully!) in his later treason trial.

Two things haunted Burr:

(1) his weak personal finances; and

(2) his killing Hamilton in their dual.

The 1800 election had a tie for Presidency between Jefferson and Burr. The U.S. House of Representatives decided in favor of Jefferson, making Burr the Vice-President.

Jefferson didn't support his Vice-President, Burr being dropped in Jefferson's second term. The most important of Burr's supporters were Secretary Gallatin and Madison (of Virginia).

After Hamilton's death, Burr became a fugitive. New York indicted him for violating the dueling laws. This was later dropped.

The basis for the treason charge was Burr's promotion of cross-border "fillibusting", an invasion by a private army without government sanction. Burn's plans had not developed an army capable of successfully invading Spanish territory in North America.

During Burr's flight, he visited Andrew Jackson at The Hermitage in Tennessee. Certainly a meeting of kindred spirits:

-   Both military officers with war experience
-   Both interested in the U.S. taking over possessions of the weakened Spanish government

Burr's treason trial started March 30, 1807. Chief Justice Marshall (presiding) ruled that Burr couldn't be tried for treason, contrary to the political wishes of President Jefferson.

Burr returned to private law practice in New York City, with his political influence nil.

If he had been selected President instead of Jefferson, the tale would have been very different!

F. Nullification Doctrine in Presidents Jackson and Bush's Terms as U.S. Presidents

The South still simmered over the 1828 tariff. John Calhoun of South Carolina drafted a formal protest against the tariff based on first principles of constitutional philosophy and calling into question the meaning of American republicanism. Calhoun denied the authority on Congress to pass tariffs for protection. He claimed that tax power is under state sovereignty. The states had the right to modify federal laws as they pertain to the states.

State elections in South Carolina in 1832 had produced a strong majority for "nullification". A convention adopted an ordinance forbidding the collection of the tariff with the boundaries on South Carolina. South Carolina threatened to secede from the Union, forcing President Jackson to act. He directed the Secretary of War to prepare for trouble. He told Poinsett (a unionist, a Jacksonian, and a South Carolinian) that he would employ force only after South Carolina had done so.

Congress quickly approved Jackson use of force in this matter. South Carolina then rescinded their nullification ordinance. South Carolina was heard from again at the start of the U.S. Civil War!

Present George Bush is using "signing statements" to assert his right to ignore or not enforce laws passed by Congress on the grounds they infringe on presidential authority or violate other constitutional provisions! His "signing statements" have challenged such items as a Congressional ban on torture, a request for data on the USA Patriot Act, whistle blower protection, and the use of U.S. troops fighting rebels in Columbia.

The Justice Department says that Bush has issued 110 signing statements compared with President Clinton's 80.

Deputy Assistant Attorney General Michelle Boardman said: "Presidential signing statements are a statement by the President explaining his interpretation of and responsibilities under the law."

The ABA task force said: "The President's constitutional duty is to enforce laws he has signed into being unless they are held unconstitutional by the Supreme Court or by a subordinate tribunal."

Note that the President's veto power is a strong tool for him.

It is not difficult to imagine what President John Quincy Adams, Chief Justice Marshall, Benjamin Franklin, President Jackson, President Lincoln and Present Franklin Roosevelt would say about this! Perhaps President Bush should be called "the nullification President".

G. The Second Seminole War

The Seminole Indians of Florida fought the hardest of all the Indian tribes against removal to Oklahoma reservations.

In a council called at Fort Gibson by the Indian agent Wiley Thompson, Osceola refused to sign the treaty and said he'd fight. This precipitated the Second Seminole War from 1835 to 1842, a game of "cat-and-mouse" in the Florida swamps against federal troops.

December 28, 1835 Osceola and his followers ambushed and killed Thompson and six others outside Fort Key.

He kept his village with its women and children deep in the swamps hidden from the federal troops. Whenever his men had an encounter with the federal troops or the white settlers, the Seminoles gave more than they received.

After two years of fighting, the Indian resources were dwindling, as they were not provisioned for continuous war like the U.S. government was. In 1837 Osceola was captured carrying a white flag of truce under U.S. General Jesup's orders.

Osceola was imprisoned in Fort Moultrie, S.C. He died within three months of captivity, supposed of malaria. His body should be exhumed and checked for traces of poison, like the signs of arsenic found in Napoleon's body when it was moved from Elba to Paris.

General Jesup broke a truce! No peace treaty was ever signed. Actually the war dragged on until 1858 when most of the Seminoles were either dead, surrendered, or moved to Oklahoma reservations.

The Second Seminole War was the most expensive war the U.S. government ever fought against Indians, and had the most troop casualties. The Indians would not sit still to be artillery targets.

H. The Natchez Trace

One of the oldest roads in the world is the Natchez Trace, covering 450 miles from Nashville, Tennessee to Natchez, Mississippi on the banks of the Mississippi River. This journey took between fifteen to twenty days. It has Indian temple mounds and village sites that existed as long ago as 8000 BC.

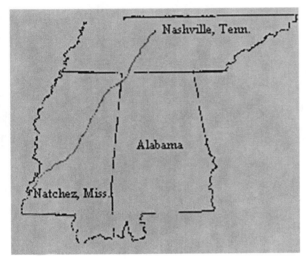

It was the only reliable and most expedient link between the goods of the North and the trading posts of Louisiana. The Indians traded and hunted along it. The Choctaw, Natchez, and Chickasaw Indians lived along this road. French traders, missionaries, and soldiers traveled over the old Indian trade route from 1649 on, perhaps traversed by Spanish explorer Hernando De Soto.

Then the "Kaintuck" flatboatmen stamped it into a road on their way back from trading their farm goods in Spanish Natchez and New Orleans. The only market place for the mountain settlers of Tennessee to sell their goods was Natchez on the banks of the Mississippi River. By 1809 the trail was fully navigable by wagon.

Traders, government officials, and soldiers made it a link between the Mississippi Territory and the newly formed United States from 1800 to 1830. In 1800 Congress extended mail service to Natchez. Inns or "stands" began popping up every few miles along the trace

And, of course, famous highwaymen (such as John Murrell and Samuel Mason) ambushed, robbed, and killed travelers, typically disemboweling them, filling their abdomens with rocks, and dumping them into creeks and swamps. "Natchez Under-The-Hill", just outside Natchez, was a haven for robbers and murders.

The Trace flourished and grew before the time of steamboats, gradually dying with their arrival.

I. *The Sims War*

Great Grandfather Lane was talking to Uncle Henry Lane (his son) one night while I was visiting. He talked about the Sims War in 1891 when a house was surrounded, set on fire, and men, women, and children were shot when they ran from the house. Grandfather was in the posse that captured the men involved, whom they lynched. He kept a piece of the hanging rope!

At the end of his talk he regretted taking the law into his own hands. There is no question that a jury would have condemned the men and the law would have legally executed them. To do it as part of a posse leaves memories not easily forgotten. What would you have done if you had been in the posse? Perhaps a deeper examination would help you make your decision.

Robert Sims fought in the Civil War and was injured by a bayonet, part remaining in his forehead. After he returned home, he was cheated out of his funds, and turned to bootlegging whisky to survive. He founded his own church with both white and black members. His followers were called "simistas" and were aggressive against other citizens in the local community.

All this came to a head in 1891. Annoyed local Choctaw County citizens reported him to the Federal authorities in Mobile, Alabama for bootlegging. The federal authorities tried to arrest him, but were afraid to fight his local supporters. He fled to Mississippi, returning to Choctaw County only after the Alabama governor vouched for his safety. He said he was going to punish the man (John McMillan) he thought had turned him in for bootlegging. One night (December 23, 1891) he and his followers surrounded the man's house and set it on fire. Men, woman, and children were shot as they fled the burning house.

A posse was organized to capture him and his followers. Some citizens hanged Jim Sims, his brother, an innocent man who came down to Choctaw County to try to help resolve the situation. They cornered Sims in his home in Bladon Springs. He surrendered to Federal authorities, who then turned him over to local citizens. Later in Mobile the head Federal Marshall said: "They couldn't be stopped". The citizens hanged Sims and his followers, and buried them hastily.

One of his "gang" confessed on the gibbet that they had killed another minister, Richard Bryant Carroll (a Baptist minister), one night at his home, and tried to kill another one. This was so far "out of line" that I can only conclude that he was insane. You can't blame an honorable family like the Sims for the actions of an insane member!

Bladon Springs, Alabama is a resort. These events are not advertised on billboards!

VI. The Civil War

A. *Grant Emerges Into History*

Some of us hear the call of destiny. For Ulysses S. Grant the Mexican War was a training period for command, and the Civil War was his rise to successful leadership. His only successes in life were in war and in writing his "Personal Memoirs".

After graduating in 1843 from the U.S. Military Academy at West Point as a 2nd lieutenant. He ranked as 21st out of 39 graduating students. He entered the U.S. Army at Jefferson Barracks in St. Louis County. He was a sloppy cadet but an excellent horseman.

He fought in the Mexican War in 1846 through 1848 under Generals Zachary Taylor and Winfield Scott. He considered the war as unjust to the Mexicans but fought anyway. He emerged from the conflict as a Captain. Mostly because of his excessive drinking, he resigned from the Army in July, 1854.

The Mexican War of 1846

He reentered the Army as a 2nd lieutenant under General Zachary Taylor.

He was detailed to act as Acquisition Master and Commissary to the regiment.

Grant compares Generals Taylor and Scot:

(1) General Taylor never wore uniforms. He moved about the battle field in which he was operating. to see himself what the situation was. He was not a conversationist, but he could express himself clearly on paper, with no regard for how "history" might judge his actions and plans. He was pleasant to serve with.

(2) General Scott also wore the correct uniform. His orders were very precise, written for the "eyes of history". He dealt more through his staff than by his own observation.

Grant's war experience was of great advantage to him afterwards:

- the many practical lessons taught
- he met and worked with nearly all the regular army regular officers,
- especially learning the characters of the Southern officers whom
- he fought against in the Civil War. He knew General Lee personally.

He fought in most major engagements of the Mexican War. He was awarded two Brevet promotions.

The Civil War of 1861-1865

He was refused a command by all normal means. He just managed election as colonel of a troublesome Illinois militia regiment. Because of the need for Army senior officers, he was promoted to brigadier general a few months later.

His chance came when his superior Halleck reluctantly ordered him to take half-finished Fort Henry on the Tennessee River. He stretched his orders and pushed on to Fort Donelson, which surrendered to him with minimal fighting. After ten months of defeats Washington was very enthusiastic and Grant was promoted major general by President Lincoln.

He was surprised at the Battle of Shiloh Church the first day by attack by the Confederates. He barely survived the first day, winning with reinforcements the next day. The casualties of the Federals were heavy, a trademark of General Grant's battles! It is fortunate for him that he was on the superior side in resources.

He chased Southern General Pemberton around Mississippi. The Battle of Champion Hill was on the rail line from Jackson to Vicksburg, where Grant was headed. This was a very bloody battle. Pemberton had a strong position on Champion Hill. After losing the battle, Pemberton took his remaining forces to take command in Vicksburg.

Grant took Pemberton's surrender at Vicksburg, splitting the Confederacy in half. Grant was made lieutenant general, a rank that only General Washington had previously held.

Grant was summoned to Washington to become overall commander.

His strengths include the coordination of the campaign of several independent armies, and his aggression and tenacity in command. General Lee out-generalled Grant, but Grant just kept coming with his superior resources. Finally he cornered Lee and forced his surrender. Remarkable is that the surrender terms were such that there were no treason trials.

The South couldn't have afforded Grant as a General. The Battle of Cold Harbor was excessively bloody, but he won! He met his destiny as a successful commander with the North's resources. As Lincoln said" "Grant fights!"–unlike General McClellan. The less said about Grant's presidency the better!

B. The Hurrah at Champion Hill

General Grant took Jackson, Mississippi. He then marched his men down the railway leading to Vicksburg, which he intended a major attack on. About 100 miles west of Jackson was a large plantation containing a large hill. The plantation was evacuated before the battle (which was fought May 16, 1863). .

Confederate Lieutenant General John C. Pemberton got there first with his men and set up a strong defense based on control of the hill.

Grant writes in his Memoirs that Pemberton had a strong position. Pemberton's position was one of the highest points in that section, and commanded the entire group in the range. In intense fighting the Federals were repulsed several times. After one repulse, the Confederates dug in on the hill stood up and yelled the Rebel battle yell. The Federals shot thousands down with their minie rifles. **This was not a football game!**

The Confederates lost 4,300 casualties to the Federals loss of about 2,500. They couldn't hold the ensuing position.

Grant writes that he could watch thousands of the enemy cut down and not feel anything emotionally. It was only after the battle that he had human compassion for the enemy killed. General Pemberton retreated with his remaining troops to Vicksberg, which he later surrendered to Grant.

The plantation was destroyed by pilferage and General Sherman's orders. The stacks of bodies of soldiers were buried in mass grades.

Pemberton was worried about possible Federal pursuit, which would probably have destroyed his forces. Grant criticizes one of his generals for not fighting with serious casualties. He felt that he could have wiped out Pemberton's forces.

Pemberton received a lot of Confederate criticisms for his generalship both at Champion Hill and at Vicksburg. Actually Pemberton was completely outclassed as a general by Grant, who was world class!

C. The "Quiet" Union General: George H. Thomas

The most impressive general in the Civil War for the modern military reader was General H. Thomas, head of the Army of the Cumberland. He "did his homework", not being a political general.

He was born in 1816 in Virginia. He won every engagement where he commanded. He taught artillery and cavalry at West Point. In the secession crisis he took the side of the North without hesitation. One famous Confederate general said he should be executed as a traitor. Not at all–he just made his choice of sides!

He was promoted to brigadier general of the regular army May 15, 1961.

The technical advances he used are impressive:

- **the techniques of economy of force**
- **the use of map coordinates in battle planning**
- **the concept of remote fire control**
- **a pioneer in the use of combined forces**
- **developed portable pontoons**
- **had the most developed telegraphy service of any army on either side**
- **with Major General McCallum he developed a movable railway base and repair center**
- **had a wide-ranging secret service with a spy network throughout the South**
- **had the Civil War's most efficient hospital service with chloroform used as regular practice**
- **established an efficient mess service with full-time cooks**
- **was the only commander under whom colored troops played a key role in a decisive Union victory**

He also equipped one of his units with the Sharps rifle (beloved of buffalo hunters). This rifle could be fired and reloaded at least three times faster than the Confederate muzzle-loading guns.

General Thomas was a McClellan in organization, but also fought! He wouldn't attack until all his preparations were completed. General Grant called him "slow in action", but General Thomas won in a devastating fashion!

General Grant believed in immediate battle action, which meant he suffered more casualties than did Thomas. Often Grant was in trouble the first day of battle, but was rescued the next day by reinforcements (as at Shiloh). Of course, Grant was a big improvement over General McClellan!

General Thomas resembles General Montgomery of World War II: neither fought until he was certain to win

D. Quantrell's Guerilla Warfare in Kansas and Missouri

Missouri had a very confused political setup when the Civil War started. Essentially, the "bushwhackers" became Confederate "irregulars". Or "guerrillas" (as we call then now). The level of violence was as high as in South Vietnam. After the War they became bandits.

William Clarke Quantrell was born in Ohio in 1837. He fought on both sides in the struggle over Kansas. He terrorized the Kansas countryside almost entirely for profit.

Setting out with his brother for California, they were ambushed by Kansas outlaws who shot them. Quantrell survived, but not his brother, He vowed to avenge the death of his brother. In the War he killed every Union soldier, and, every male Kansan he could lay his hands on.

Just before the Civil War started, he shifted his operations to Missouri. He started with 15 men, and never exceeded a hundred. After the War started, he and his men were sworn into the Confederate Army, and he was given the rank of Captain.

On March 22, 1861 after learning the Union General Halleck decreed the execution of captured guerrillas, he personally shot one of his prisoners. He ordered his men to "give no quarter" to captured Union solders.

At Lawrence, Kansas Quantrell and his men committed one of the worst atrocities of the war, killing every man and boy encountered. This resembles the Vietnamese "Tet Offensive", except the Vietnamese had lists of which men to kill for political reasons.

He was "bushwhacked" in Kentucky May 19, 1865, and died of his wounds.

E. Fighting Guerrillas in Missouri

Before, during, and after the Civil War guerrillas were active destructively. In Missouri they were known as the "Bushwackers".

On August 30, 1861, Federal Commander General John C. Fremont declared martial law in Missouri. He warned that civilians aiding the rebellion would be shot. President Lincoln insisted that no civilian would be shot without a White House review of each case.

For the first time in American history military commissions began to prosecute U.S. citizens. By the end of the war, Missouri had 46.2% of all the recorded military trials of civilians.

In 1862 Major General Henry W. Halleck (the successor to Fremont) cooperated with the provisional government in creating a local force that would be the primary response force for pacifying the state. It was called the Missouri State Militia (MSM), and could only be used within Missouri's borders.

The military rapidly began to supplant civil government in many areas of life. The Army enforced a loyalty oath, and put the press under strict censorship.

General Halleck issued General Order # 32 on December 22, 1861: "anyone caught in the act of sabotage will be immediately shot.". At the end of 1861 he had his regiments start to destroy or disburse the guerrilla squads.

To a limited degree the marching, fighting, and harsh measures only weeded out the week and disorganized insurrectionists. Small bands continued a more skillful guerrilla struggle.

Under the pressure of the Union counter-offensive, the secessionist guerrillas broke into small cells that fought without central direction or official Confederate sanctions. These guerrillas were called "Bushwackers".

On April 25, 1863 Brigadier General Thomas Ewing, Jr. issued General Order # 11: "Everyone living in the counties in his district and bordering Kansas were ordered to leave within 15 days". The area depopulated by Order # 11 became known as the "Burnt Region". The order aroused pity in the minds of Union soldiers, but no guilt.

These Federal measures had their effectiveness, but the guerrillas responded and continued to fight.

VII. Genealogy

A. Genealogical Brickwalls

Searching backwards for my ancestors
Gets more difficult approaching 1500;
Most have similar first names
Such as Henry and William.

My Bonner and Champion ancestors
Came to America from England
To the Isle of Wight in Virginia
And Chowan in North Carolina.

It was not unusual for men
To have two or three wives;
No divorces, so either they wore
Out or died during childbirth.

A Binn connection leads
To a Scottish king.
I'm not impressed by
Relation to a Scottish king!

The dates of their births and deaths
Vary from source to source;
Not to mention Campion becoming
Champion and Boner Bonner.

Records diminish in quality and quantity
Before 1500, not to mention
Surnames not so often used
In the twelfth century.

Tracing in England to
Viking lines is only possible
If related to Norman nobility;
Most Vikings didn't keep records!

Why did my ancestors
Leave England for America?
Some of possible reasons follow:
Political persecution,

Religious persecution, crime
Conviction and transportation,
Looking for cheap Indian lands,
Being evicted from their farmlands.

I'm having difficulties finding
Life details of my English ancestors;
Are letters and family histories
Only available at English sites?

On GenForum a correspondent
Mentions there are many Bonners and
Champions in Scotland and Ireland;
They must be hiding from me!

I know that some of my English ancestors
Were indentured in Virginia and North Carolina;
Data is hard to find; is indenturing
Considered shameful by later generations?

Another correspondent mentions that
Our lines has as many bastards as
The Windsors ruling in England today;
How do I follow such lines?

I've done a DNA test for the Y-chromosome
To trace back on the fathers; No mentions
of thirty-seven matches indicates
There aren't common ancestors.

A genealogical "brickwall" might take me
Six months or a year to resolve;
I'll have to live to one-hundred
To trace to the Norman Invasion!

Don't be selfish when
Naming your children;
Make it easy for your
Dependents to search genealogy!

B. DNA Testing

Chromosomes are threadlike strands composed of DNA, the molecule that carries genetic information. They are hidden deep inside the DNA. Chromosomes carry genes, which are sections of DNA that make up the building plans for physical traits.

In humans, chromosomes come in pairs. You have 22 pairs of uniquely shaped autosomal chromosomes plus 1 pair of sex chromosomes, for a total of 23 chromosome pairs. Sex is determined by two sex chromosomes, X and Y. Females have two X chromosomes, while males have one X and one Y chromosome. Since Y doesn't recombine with other chromosomes, it is good for tracing how men have traveled and settled around the world.

Haplotype stands for an inventory of human alleles (alternative forms of genes), defined by a series of markers that are shared by other men who carry the same random mutations in the "junk DNA". The alleles are single base pair changes (SNP), the result of thousands of substitution mutations. Collectively these changes vary enough for geneticists to discover each population's genetic signature. Geneticists create genetic maps that relate SNP alleles to geographical locations.

A lot of "junk DNA" gets translated into RNA. "junk DNA" actually carries out important functions that regulate how organizations are put together. RNA is the single-stranded molecules that transfer information carried by DNA to the protein-manufacturing part of cells.

I chose to have Y-chromosome DNA testing in National Geographic's "Genographic Project". The ultimate goal of the project is to line up haplotypes to populations, along with information about the environment, family history, and medical conditions to develop tailor-made treatment for diseases. The test cost $99, and involved rubbing swabs on the inside of my cheeks.

From this I received a certificate of Y-chromosome DNA testing. I am a member of Haplogroup R1b (M343). Haplogroup **R1b** (marker M343) comprises roughly 70 percent of the men in southern England. In parts of Spain and Ireland the number exceeds 90 percent. My family history shows that the Champions (Father's line) were in England 500 years ago. They started to migrate in the 1600's to Virginia and North Carolina in the American colonies.

Marker genes show the paths of migration of your ancestors. A marker is a gene mutation, random, naturally occurring, and usually harmless. It can be mapped through generations because it will be passed down from the man to whom it occurs to every male in his line for thousands of years. When geneticists identify such a marker, they try to figure out when it first occurred, and in which geographic region of the world.

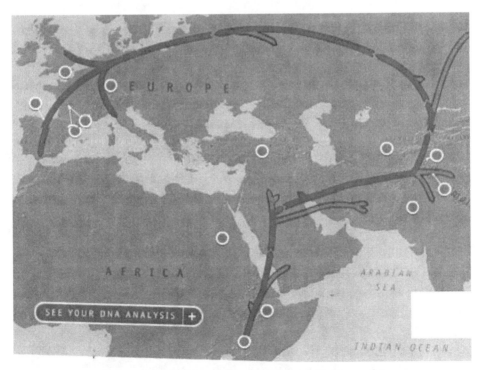

Genographic Map from National Geographic

M168 > M89 > M9 > M45 .> M207 > M173 > M343

Identifications:

M168 is my earliest ancestor about 50,000 years ago in northeast Africa in the region of the Rift Valley

M89 is moving through Northern Africa or the Middle East 45.000 years ago following the expanding grasslands and plentiful game in the Middle East

M9 is the Eurasian clan spreading wide and far 40,000 years ago in Iran or southern Central Asia

M45 is the Journey through Central Asia 35,000 years ago in Central Asia; because the glaciers of the Ice Age began to expand once again; my ancestors followed the herds of game north

M207 is Leaving Central Asia 30,000 years ago to head west towards the European sub-continent; during this period the climate fostered a land rich in resources and opened a window into Europe on the Eurasian steppelands

M173 is Colonizing Europe as the first modern Europeans 30,000 years age; about 20,000 years ago expanding ice sheets forced my ancestors to move south to Spain, Italy, and to the Balkans; about 12,000 years ago the ice retreated and temperatures became warmer, so many descendants of M173 moved north again to recolonize places that had become inhospitable during the Ice Age

M343 is Direct Descendants of Cro-Magnon 30,000 years ago in Western Europe

What a travelogue over the last 50,000 years! At the last two markers, the travelers were working around the ice glaciers in Europe.

PBS Home Video's "Journey of Man" cdrom shows the actual paths of (a) the Sen people (pigmies) from Africa to Australia (to become the aborigines). (b) The migration to central Asia, and then to Europe of my ancient ancestors (cro-magnon). (c) The migration of Siberian natives to the New World across the Bering "land-bridge".

Other uses of the results are:

(1) Adding the data to a family database for further research.

(2) Finding out about other individuals now living with similar haplotypes in worldwide populations to see if you have common ancestors. This can be done on the Internet;

(3) DNA fingerprinting (in 1985 a team of scientists in Britain figured out how to profile to a tiny bit of DNA uniqueness from junk DNA into a DNA fingerprint). These have even been taken from Egyptian mummies.

C. Practical Uses of DNA

Today DNA has many practical uses, with the medical uses continuing to expand in the future.

Genealogical Research

DNA can be used in genealogical research in databases of DNA of related males. Retrieval of so-called ancient DNA is being done, with special attention paid to contamination. Several families have DNA databases if their family. Check "GENFORUM" on the Internet for your family.

DNA contains the ultimate forensic record of evolution (genomics). Each step in evolution is taken and recorded in DNA. Each change or new trait is due to one or more stepwise changes in DNA which are traceable. Natural selection acts only on what is useful for the moment.

"Markers" are used in the National Geographic DNA database ("The Genographic Project) to show a path of migration of your ancestors from Africa to Europe (in my case). Anthropologists organize the Y-chromosomes into branches called Haplogroups.

The genetic markers are mutations in the DNA (usually harmless) and act as beacons. They can be mapped through generations because it will be passed from the man in whom it occurs to his son, then to their sons and to every male in his family for thousands of years. When geneticists identify such a marker they try to figure where it first occurred and in which geographic region of the world. This is discussed in Chapter VI ("Genealogy"), Section B ("DNA Testing").

Family Tree (www.familytreedna.com) analyzed my Y-DNA results. The examinations placed me in Haplogroup **R1b1.** I had seven matches on 37 markers. You are given the names and Email addresses of those participants who have agreed for their results to be public. I send them copies of my family genealogy charts and we consulted. We couldn't find a common ancestor (MLCA–the most recent common ancestor). Many people sharing a surname will often have a perfect or near perfect match on 37 markers. Consider joining the free International Society of Genetic Genealogy at www.isogg.org.

As knowledge of the human genome advances, other information could be extracted from DNA samples, including physical traits like race. British researchers are looking for the possibility of obtaining physical indications such as skin and hair color, height, and sex. If enough markers are used, a researcher can reasonably state to which of the major continental races (Africa, Caucasian, East Asian, or American Indian) a person sampled is a member of. as well as the percentage of such ancestry in the case of people of mixed races.

Well-known DNA evidence seekers for innocence of people accused of crimes:

(1) The Court of Last Resort (directed by Earl Stanley Gardner); and

(2) The Innocence Project at the Benjamin N. Cordoso School of Law at Yeshiva University.

Medical Aspects of DNA

Your DNA can forewarn you of possible future medical problems for you. There are tests for specific ailments available to the public. It is hoped that rapid diagnosis of disease will occur, with treatments tailored to your individual genetic makeup to have maximum effects on you with minimum side-effects.

This could make possible a dramatic shift toward preventative medicine. Americans have private medical insurance and might not have incentives to invest in genetic tests that help with prevention.

Your Employer and Your Insurance Want to Examine Your DNA!

Insurance companies are worried they will be put out of business, being left with only the customers who have reason to believe they will need to make a claim at some time.

Insurance companies are very interested in the results of genetic tests. The tests show how a particular individual's policy is likely to be profitable for the insurance company.

Genetic data could be used by insurance firms to discriminate against those with higher rates of certain diseases.

Americans are overwhelming in favor of a law protecting genetic privacy. If genetic information is kept secret from insurance companies and individuals are free to add or drop insurance coverage, the problem of adverse selection may occur.

Once you have perfect information, it will be the death of insurance, which depends on uncertainty and pooled risks.

Social outcry over a growing class of uninsurables might make the Government the insurer of last resort.

Genetic Counseling

Engaged couples may seek genetic counseling before marriage. First, a family tree must be drawn, noting every inheritable disease of their ancestors.

Medical problems include:
- cancer
- alcoholism or drug addition
- mental illness or retardation
- heart disease, high blood pressure, or stroke
- asthma

- kidney disease
- birth defects, miscarriages, or still births

Genetic counselors must look for very subtle signs to detect particular patterns of inheritance in humans. The particular ways in which human genetic disorders are passed should be established.

DNA Evidence in Crime Scene Investigations

Forensic genetics is the exploration of DNA evidence. DNA fingerprints (DNA profiling) are the process identifying the patterns within the DNA scene:

(1) Confirm that a person was present at a particular location

(2) Determine identity and genders

(3) Assign paternity

In 1985 a group of British scientists discovered how to take a tiny bit of DNA uniqueness into a DNA fingerprint. Even a skin cell has enough DNA to make a fingerprint. Of course, samples must be taken carefully. Even plants have a space in the DNA evidence game.

With DNA fingerprinting, you can calculate the odds of another person having the same pattern.

In 1990 the FBI set up its DNA database, CODIS (combined DNA index system). By June, 2002 it contained 1,013,746 DNA fingerprints. To be really effective, everyone should contribute a DNA fingerprint!

In order for the Reader to gain an appreciation of the expertise and imagination required in such cases, let us examine the case of **Anastasia:**

In July, 1918, Czar Nicholas of Russia, his wife, and three (of four) daughters were killed by the Bolsheviks on the Lenin's orders. It was thought that his son Alexis was killed elsewhere, but that his daughter Anastasia might have survived.

A woman in Sweden claimed to be the real Anastasia. If true and proven, she would have inherited a fortune from the Czar's resources held outside Russia. Her proof was not satisfactory, and she died without inheriting.

In 1979 a mass grave in Siberia was discovered, and later it was exhumed. To identify the Czar they had to use two distant relatives and Georgij Romanov, brother of the Czar. Anna Russell had been cremated, which cannot give a DNA sample. Fortunately, while alive she had an emergency operation at a Swedish hospital, and some of her tissues were still usable. The doctor used a DNA fingerprinting method with mitochondrial DNA (mtDNA), which proved conclusively that Anna had not been related to the Czar.

This investigation and analysis exhibited a high level of professional technique and imagination!

D. My Bonner Genealogy

My Mother's line is Bonner and they came from England to Virginia first (to what is now North Carolina). There is a Bonner Surname DNA Project directed by Gregg Bonner at:

gbonner@unich.edu

I drew a chart with all my known grandparents. I could go as far as Great-Grandparents. I went to the free Mormon internet site to check out names and birth-death dates. You can join it. They have many centers around the country where you can get assistance.

I have found the Ancestry.com database very easy to use and cheap at about $100 for a year's subscription. Cheaper (but still good) is the Godfrey Library (on the internet at godfrey.org). They have many Online Databases. You can get a Library Card for use on the Internet for $35 a year.

I obtained copies of the Bonner Family Bible from a Bonner relative. I also got a copy of a book written on the Bonners.

I find that tracing back my relatives gets difficult in the 1500's (in England). Of course, you can check English sites for genealogy.

Following is my line for Bonners going back to 1500, but the detail is less the further you go back in history! Sooner or later you may reach "brick walls" in your sources. It didn't help that the Bonners use certain given names over and over again. For example, Henry Bonner ("The Navigator") was the first of four Henry's in a row in North Carolina!

A good genealogical drawing software package is "Family Tree". Their magazine ("Family tree Magazine") is good. Another genealogical magazine is "Family Chronicle".

My corroboration is the wife's given name. Children's names are also good.

I use a "Personal Pedigree" based on the male Y-chromosome passing from father to son throughout generations. This is designed for rapid penetration in my research into the past.

My Bonner Personal Ancestry (Personal Pedigree):

Ralph Bonner b. 1585 England .m Emma Baker Maulden

Henry Bonner b. 1620 England .m 1639 migrated 1664
d. 1689 N.C. .m Mary Grabham

Henry Bonner b. 1650 England d. 1716 N.C.
.m Ruth Martin

Colonel Henry Bonner .b 1679 N.C. d. 1738 N.C.
.m Deborah Whitley 1689-1728 N.C.

Henry Bonner .b 1708 N.C. d, 1766 N.C.
.m Sarah Luten (1st wife) b 1700 N.C.

Thomas Bonner .b 1744 N.C. d. 1804 GA .m Margaret A. Jones
b. 1750 (NC)-1828 (GA)

Jordan Bonner 1767 (GA)-1841 (AL) .Rachel Moon (2nd wife,
my line)

Seaborn Bonner I 1800 (AL)–1874 (AL)
.m Mary Martin (.m 1837)

Seaborn Bonner II 1849 (AL)-1922 (AL)
.m Elizabeth Boney (.m 1871)

Seaborn Bonner III 1888 AL)–1964 (AL)
.m Lillie Mae Lane 1871-1955

S.L. Bonner (my Mother) .b 1918-1991 AL .m William
Ralph Champion, Sr. .b 1912 MS d. 1941 AL

William Ralph Champion, Jr. (me!)
b. 1938, Still living

E. Henry Bonner: Migrating from England to Virginia

Prominent reasons for migrating were: (1) the availability of cheap land in the colonies; (2) religious persecution in England; (3) only the first son getting land inheritance in England.

Henry Bonner ("The Navigator") was my line's pioneer in migrating from Bristol, England to Virginia (in a part that later became North Carolina). He was born in England in 1617 in the Bristol area. His father was Ralph Bonner. His mother was Emma Baker Maulden. Bristol was the main port of London.

He made a voyage to Virginia Colony in 1660-1662. He returned to England for his family and returned to Virginia before 1664. This was about the time that the "Black Plague" was again active in London. He apparently served a period of indenture, and is next heard of in 1680 in Albemarle County in Virginia (later to be North Carolina).

He died in 1689 in Chowan Precinct (now in North Carolina). His wife was Katherine. Their children were: (1) Henry, born in England 1664, died 1738 in North Carolina; (2)William, born before 1664, died 1728 in North Carolina; and (3) Thomas, born in Virginia in 1664, died 1685 in North Carolina.

F. Jordan Bonner: Migrating from North Carolina to Alabama

A pattern of early Western migration followed the expansion of the plantation system of agriculture. The magnet which attracted this was the presence of cheap, abundant land in a virgin wilderness. Most of this land was taken from the Indians one way or another.

I will use my ancestor Jordan Bonner to illustrate this migration process.

Jordan Bonner was the second son of Thomas Bonner (1744-1805). Jordan was born 1768 in North Carolina, dying in 1841 in Choctaw County, Alabama (where I was raised).

He moved to Clarke County, Georgia, with his father and brothers. He married three wives: (1) Mary Martin, who died with their child in a fire; (2) Rachel Moon (my line) with seven children, one of which was my ancestor Seaborn Lafayette Bonner; (3) Polly Adams with twelve children. You can get an idea of the progeny by looking at the items for "Jordan Bonner (1769-1841) Children???" on the Internet in "genforum" for the Bonner family.

My cousin, Alma Roberts, wrote "The Jordan Bonner Family History", in which I am listed!

Jordan Bonner owned much land in Georgia as late as 1809. In 1807, for example, he bought land in the 1807 Land Lottery of Georgia. This was formerly Indian land. He left Georgia in 1811 for Alabama. Given his numerous children, it is not surprising that I am related to most of the people living in the area around Toxey, Choctaw County, Alabama!

Note the process of selling land where he lived, only to buy new land in a new area (usually in former Indian lands).

G. My Champion Genealogy

My Father's line came from England to the county of Virginia called "Isle of Wight". It is on the James River, but in a healthier location than Jamestown. There is a Champion DNA Project at:

worldfamilies.net/surnames/c/champion/pats.html

My Personal Pedigree (my male line only)

Edward Campion, b. Eng .m Martha Elizabeth Fields

Edward Champion, Sr. .b 1609 Bristol, Eng migrated 1635
d. 1668, Isle of Wight, VA .m Elizabeth Atkins (1610-?)

Edward Champion, Jr. b. 1635 Isle of Wight, VA d. 1668, NC
.m Priscilla Moore

Benjamin Champion, Jr. b. 1660 Isle of Wight, Virginia d. 1735
Surry County, VA .m Elizabeth Williams b. 1664 Isle of Wight,
VA d. 1736, VA

John Champion b. 1705 Surry County, VA d. 1757 .m Susannah?
b. 1710, Surry County, VA

Charles Champion b. 1735 North Carolina d. 1791, NC
.m Ann Carroll b. 1714 NC d. 1737 NC

John Champion b. 1760 NC, d. 181? MS
.m Temperance Harris b. 1841 TN

John Champion b. 1790 NC d. 1861
.m Nancy Hannah b. 1795 NC

William J. Champion b. 1817 NC
. m Melinda? b. 1836 TN

Alexander Champion .b 1851 GA d. 1910 MS
    m. Sarah Rebecca Fox b. 1851
    d. 1929 MS

John William Champion b. 1880 d. 1952 MS
    .m Myrtle Irene Owen b. 1886 d. 1951
    MS

William Ralph Champion, Sr. b. 1912
    MS d. 1941 AL
    .m S.L. Bonner b. 1918 d. 1991
    AL

William Ralph Champion, Jr. (me!)
    b. 1938 MS, still living

VIII. Miscellaneous

A. Outrageous Surmises:

What we know to be true at one time may later be proven false. Following are surmises I make for further investigation:

Surmise 1:   Homo Sapiens and Neanderthals interacted and cohabited with children.

In June 2003 a jaw and a skull with mixed Homo Sapiens and Neanderthal features was discovered in a deep cave in the Rumanian Carpathian Mountains.

Surmise 2:   Stalin sometimes gave Russian Orthodox services disguised in Moscow while he was General Secretary of the Communist Party of the Soviet Union.

He had been trained in Georgia to be a Russian Orthodox priest. He didn't totally destroy religion in Russia, nor destroy all churches. He occasionally uttered religious phases such as "As God pleases".

Surmise 3:   Oil has a source other than just the decay of ancient forests. It may have a purpose in this living earth of tectoral plates. Present oil wells may be refreshed with oil from sources we don't know about.

My predictions: (1) oil will be found in Antarctica; (2) when oil has been mostly removed from under the Middle East, the space will be filled with water, structural collapses and earthquakes occurring.

Surmise 4:   As the Solar System goes about its 240 million year orbit around the Milky Way Galaxy, some areas of this journey are more dangerous than others. If the Earth is 3 million years old, it would have made 12 tours with the Sun around the galaxy. Can these critical positions be identified by positions in the Galaxy and Earth time periods? And used for predictive purposes?

Surmise 5:   Is evolution based on mutation, rather than Darwin's "Origin of the Species" theories? How can you decide when a mutation has survived? How might mankind mutate in the next 100,000 years?:

Surmise 6:   When South America separated from Africa and moved on a platonic plate to where it is now, was there passage of prehuman life? Could archeology off the African coast support this? Could these hominids have developed to homo sapiens in the trip to where South America now is, or after the journey ended?

Surmise 7:   What would have happened if the South had reached a draw with the North in the Civil war?

               They would just have had another war later, which the North would probably have won since they would have gotten stronger militarily.

Surmise 8:   How successful would Grant have been fighting for the South?

               General Grant always pressed for action, disregarding casualties for results. Fighting for the militarily weaker side, he would not have been "saved" by reinforcements.

Credits for Images and Maps:

- "karenswhimsey.com" public domain web site for a public domain image of Osceola.

- National Park Service for a public domain map of the Natchez Trace

- Ohio History Central, October 11, 2007, www.ohiohistorycenreal.org/image.php?img=1088 for a portrait of Tecumseh

- Portrait of Bartolomew Gosnold was commissioned by the Author From Lincoln Park Studio, who announces it is now in the public domain

- Text and map of my personal Genographic Haplogroup results by permission of © 2005-2006 National Geographic Society. THE GENOGRAPHIC PROJECT, NATIONAL GEOGRAPHIC, and Yellow Border are trademarks of NGS. All rights reserved.

- The College of New Jersey (teachpol.tcnj.edu) for a public domain Bust of Aaron Burr

- The Perry-Castenada Library at the University of Texas at Austin for public domain portrait of Pocahontas, public domain maps of Jamestown Settlement and Roanoke Island, and an image of Captain John Smith from a map of New England.

- Wikimedia for public domain maps of Jamestown and Roanoke Island

- www.army.mil for a public domain image of the Jamestown Fort

Bibliography

Brands, H.W.: "Andrew Jackson: His Life and Times", Anchor Books, 2001, ISBN 1-4000-3072-2

Carroll, Sean: "The Making of the Fittest: DNA and the Ultimate Frontier Record of Evolution", W.W. Norton and Company, 2006, ISBN 978-0-393-33051-9

Cawthorne, Nigel: "A History of Pirates: Blood and Thunder on the High Seas", Chartwell Books, Inc., 2003, ISBN 13-978-0-7858-1856-4

Current World Archaeology No. 4: "Oase Case: The Discovery of Europe's Oldest Humans" pages 32-41

Diamond, Jared: "Guns, Germs, and Steel: The Fates of Human Societies", W. W. Norton & Company, 1999, 1997, ISBN 0-393-31755-2

Edmunds, R. David: "Tecumseh and the Quest for Indian Leadership", Longman, 1984, ISBN 0-673-39336-5

Gay, Ann Harwell: "The Perverse Prophet and Choctaw County's Sims War"

Grant, Ulysses S.: "Personal Memoirs", Penguin Books, 1999, ISBN 0-14-04, 3701 0

Isenberg, Nancy: "Fallen Founder: The Life of Aaron Burr", Viking, 2007, ISBN 978-0-670-06352-9.

Jones, Martin: "Molecule Hunt: Archeology and the Search for Ancient DNA", Arcade Publishing, 2001, ISBN 1-55970-611-2

Kenyon, T. Douglas (editor): "Forbidden History", Bear & Company, 2003, ISBN 1-59143-045-3

Kupperman, Karen Ordahl (editor): "Captain John Smith: A Select Edition of His Writings", University of North Carolina, 1988, ISBN 0-8078-1778-3

Langguth, A.J.: "Union 1812", Simon & Schuster, 2006, ISBN 13-978-0-7432-2618-9

Mahon, John K.: "History of the Second Seminole War 1835-1842 (Revised Edition)", University of Florida Press: Gainesville, 1985, ISBN 0-8130-1097-7

Mann, Charles: "1491: New Revelations of the Americas before Columbus", Alfred A. Knopf, 2006, ISBN 1-4000-40006-1

Neblock, Lucy Nita (Bonner): "The Bonner Legacy: A History of Some of the Bonners", A & L Computing, Publishers, 1999

Price, David A.: "Love and Hate in Jamestown", Alfred A. Knopf, 2003, ISBN 0-375-41541-6

Roberts, Alma: "The Jordan Bonner Family History"

Taylor, Dale: "The Writer's Guide to Everyday Life in Colonial America from 1607-1783", Writer's Digest Books, 1997, ISBN 0-89879-772-1

Thomas, Hugh: "Rivers of Gold: The Rise of the Spanish Empire from Columbus to Magellan", Random House, 2005, ISBN 0-8129-7055-1

The Economist: "Briefing: Genetics, Medicine and Insurance: Do not ask or do not Answer", pages 69-71, August 25, 2007

Ward, Christopher: "The War of the Revolution", Konecky & Konecky, 1952, ISBN 1-56852-576-1

Wilson, Harold C.: "Gosnold's Hope: The Story of Bartholomew Gosnold", Tudor Publishing, 2000, ISBN 0-936389-81-8

978-0-595-48252-8
0-595-48252-X

Printed in the United States
128290LV00002B/55/P